Top Dog

Top Dog

Marketing Yourself For Sales Success

Lee Molony

iUniverse, Inc.
New York Lincoln Shanghai

Top Dog
Marketing Yourself For Sales Success

iUniverse books may be ordered through booksellers or by contacting:

iUniverse
2021 Pine Lake Road, Suite 100
Lincoln, NE 68512
www.iuniverse.com
1-800-Authors (1-800-288-4677)

ISBN: 978-0-595-43693-4 (pbk)
ISBN: 978-0-595-88027-0 (ebk)

Printed in the United States of America

To Ev, my husband and best friend, who is my greatest fan

and

To our daughters, Laura, Kristy & Sara, who encouraged me in my creative journey.

Acknowledgments

I thank:

Eileen Keymel, without whose tireless editing *Top Dog* would not be what it is. She is a superb editor and has become a dear friend.

Veronica Keymel, an excellent artist who gave form to Top Dog and his world.

Fred Gregory, the reader of the first manuscript, who gave advice and encouragement. The book has come a long way since that early draft.

Judith Willis, who told me that I needed to write this book. She was right.

Kathie Balentine, who helped me search for a publisher. Her ongoing interest and forever friendship buoyed my spirits.

Contents

INTRODUCTION

WHY DO I WANT TO READ THIS BOOK?

If you are one of the 99.99% of salespeople who are "made," not born, or even just in the process of being "made," this book was written for you.

If you are a salesperson who fights rejection every day, who worries about meeting goal, who looks at the phone and sees a 200-pound stone, this book was written for you.

If you are an entrepreneur who just wants to do what you do well and wishes you didn't have to sell your services, in fact would rather have a tooth extracted without Novocaine than sell, this book was written for you.

If you can't find enough eager prospects who want to, or can, buy your services, this book was written for you.

Now that you know you are in the right place, let me tell you what this book will and won't do for you.

It will not give you:

   49 guaranteed closes
   23 unbeatable opening questions

15 powerhouse sales scripts
37 proven cold call techniques

It won't give you any of the traditional sales training tactics because buyers today are too sophisticated and savvy to be manipulated. They can see a sales technique coming a mile away. They have memorized the script and know what the sales-man is going to say.

That's why the "unbeatable," "guaranteed" sales techniques usually don't work. Even if they do work they have some major failings.

* They irritate, even anger, the prospect.
* They don't help you find people who want to talk to you, let alone buy from you.
* They don't help you handle that kicked-in-the-gut feeling that comes when you are rejected.
* They don't show you how to build repeat business and referral business.
* They don't show you how to get prospects to call you and ask to do business with you. (That's right. Call you and ask you to let them do business with you!)

That is why this book won't give you any "guaranteed" sales training techniques. Instead, it will show you how to:

* market yourself for sales success.
* create a product that your prospects want.
* find the best prospects for you.
* handle rejection.
* get more appointments.
* close more sales.
* keep more customers.
* get more business from current customers.
* get more referrals—even from people who aren't, and may never be, your customers.
* sell more easily.
* enjoy the process.

But, how can this book promise sales success if it isn't about selling?
If it isn't about how to sell, what the heck is it about? It is about marketing.

So often we hear people use the words marketing and selling interchangeably, but these words are not synonymous. Marketing is an all-encompassing, on-going strategy. Selling is one small piece of marketing.

Marketing makes selling possible.
Marketing creates sales opportunities.
Marketing increases client satisfaction.
Marketing creates the prospect relationship.
Marketing makes the product attractive and desirable.
Marketing makes the market desire the product.

The sale is an event. The relationship of selling to marketing is like the relationship of the wedding to the courtship and the marriage. Boy meets girl. Boy asks girl out. Boy impresses girl. Boy asks girl out on a second date. Boy makes girl happy. This goes on through the third, fourth, fifth dates, etc., etc. Marketing is what keeps the girl going out with the boy until the BIG DAY when he proposes.

The proposal is the sales call. He asks for the order. She says "Yes" or "No" or "I'll think about it." The sale is the event. Marketing is everything that leads up to it.

Marketing is also everything that comes after it. He asks. She says, "Yes." They get married. At that point marketing comes back into play. Marketing is what keeps them together until their first anniversary, second, third, fourth, etc., etc. Boy makes girl happy. Girl makes boy happy. They nurture their relationship. Boy and girl eventually celebrate their 50th wedding anniversary.

The sale is at the center of everything you do, but it is an event. Marketing makes the event possible. Marketing after the sale makes more and more events possible. Marketing makes you a desirable product. Marketing keeps you a desirable product.

If you market well, the sales will come. Inevitably. And come and come. You create an irresistible force. You cannot fail. That's right. Cannot fail. When you are talking to the right market, a market that needs you and wants you and can afford you and can have you, the sale is a foregone conclusion. THIS BOOK WILL SHOW YOU HOW TO FIND THAT MARKET, HOW TO MAKE THAT MARKET WANT YOU AND HOW TO KEEP YOUR NEW CUSTOMERS COMING BACK AND BRINGING THEIR FRIENDS WITH THEM.

It is more fun and a lot easier to sell to people who want to buy from you than to try to sell to people who don't. When you finish this book, you will have the tools to find those people and sell to them, over and over and over again.

Born salespeople enjoy selling because they are successful and believe their success will be repeated again and again. They are happy, their customers are happy and their bank accounts are happy. By using the techniques they use, you will be happy, too.

The difference between the "born salesman" and the rest of is like the difference between the frontiersman and the settler. The frontiersman was a woodsman who had a wanderlust and a thirst for adventure. He licked his lips at the mere prospect of shooting a grizzly bear. The settler, on the other hand, did what he had to do to put food on the table. He went where he had to go and did what he had to do, but he wasn't "itchin'" to hunt bears and fight Indians and malaria and starvation. He'd just as soon have been comfortable and safe, rocking on his porch in Williamsburg, Virginia or Pittsfield, Massachusetts.

But, he couldn't afford to buy land there, so he did what he had to do. He moved to the frontier and built a good life for himself and his family. So can you. You may not be a "born" salesperson, but you can still be a darn good one.

The good life is attainable in sales, but selling isn't easy. That's why I wrote this book: TO MAKE THE PROCESS OF SELLING EASIER AND MORE PROFITABLE FOR YOU.

Selling is work, but it is a lot less work to do it using a system. You need a system to be a success. We each have a finite resource pool. We have a limited amount of time, money and energy. How often have you been told, "Work hard?" That's great advice, but hard work alone won't get you where you want to go. You can work just as hard at becoming a failure as you can at becoming a success. The key to building a successful business is to leverage your resources. Work smarter, not harder.

Working smarter means having a system and working it. As a marketing consultant my goal is to help you be the top dog in your market. Hence, my system is named the Top Dog System or TDS for short.

What picture do the words "top dog" conjure up in your mind? To me, Top Dog is the lead dog in a pack. All the dogs know who Top Dog is. Even as children we all knew who Top Dog was. You wanted to play on his baseball team or eat at her lunch table.

In people packs, the top dog is not always the person with the title. He or she is always the person with the power. Everyone knows who the top dog is. (Top Dog can be male or female. For the sake of the flow of the text, whenever you read "he," please see "he or she.")

We all want to do business with Top Dog. While the others are running around in circles, chasing their tails, Top Dog knows where he is going. He doesn't strut, doesn't do a whole lot of barking and he doesn't beg for scraps. Instead, the top dog in any market just quietly, confidently, projects an aura of success that attracts prospects and turns them into clients. People want to do business with the best.

WHAT DOES THE TOP DOG SYSTEM LOOK LIKE?

The Top Dog System, TDS, has seven parts. The parts are interlocked, building upon one another. Since it is a system, you can't skip any part. Fortunately, each part you complete makes the next part easier to do. A lot of salespeople do some of the parts all of the time, but not all of the parts all of the time. They are the salespeople who eventually give up selling and go into "safe" jobs or who sell enough to survive, but not to thrive. Top Dog does all of the parts.

These are the seven parts of TDS.

Part One: Defining the product (Writing your pedigree)
In this step you will write the specifications for an irresistible product—you.

Part Two: Finding your market (Barking up the right tree)
In this step you will research possible markets and select the best market—for you.

Part Three: Getting to know your market (Studying their pedigrees)
In this step you will get to know your market even better than it knows itself.

Part Four: Introducing yourself to your market. (Barking up a storm)
In this step you will package yourself and take yourself to market.

Part Five: Approaching your market (Entering the show ring)
In this step you will approach your prospects.

Part Six: Making the sale. (Becoming the pick of the litter)
In this step you will close the sale and finally be Top Dog, the sought-after sales professional.

Part Seven: Mining your assets (Collecting bones)
In this step you will build long-lasting client relationships and leverage both client and prospect relationships to build a 100% referral business.

Once you start using the system, it actually is fun. Who wouldn't enjoy hearing the modern equivalent of the old-fashioned ringing cash register? TDS was created to make your cash register ring merrily.

CHAPTER ONE

DEFINING THE PRODUCT

Part One of TDS is Defining the Product, or, in Top Dog terms, *Writing Your Pedigree*. Your pedigree tells the world what you are. In a popular TV commercial we heard, "Parts is parts." Of course, we all know that, in selling, as in chickens and just about everything else in life, parts are not parts. Everyone is unique. TDS helps you identify what makes you unique.

What are you? What are you selling? The essence of Part One is defining you, the product. When I coach salespeople, born, made or being made, I meet initial resistance right here, at the git-go. They want to market everything to everybody. Sooner or later they sadly discover that you can't market a non-entity, a "me-too," a look-alike and that's what the vast majority of salespeople try to do. To be successful, you must market a singularly unique product. That's why TDS begins by helping you uncover and market your unique blend of talents. In the end, that's what each of us sells. The only thing we sell. I sell me and you sell you.

In an article about Richard Branson, the CEO of Virgin Atlantic Airways, the New York Times used this headline: "Of all he sells, he sells himself the best." The beauty is that each of us is selling "the best." It would be impossible, in the whole world, to find a better "you." Top Dog is always the best. So are you. Let's see how.

A business always begins marketing a product by identifying the product's USP, its unique selling proposition. In your business, you are the product. So, you need to find your USP.

What are you? You are a unique combination of personality, experience and education. You are your values. You are what you know and whom you know. These are your assets. If you were a widget, your assets would be called your product specifications.

To begin to define you, the product, you have to list all of your product specifications, your assets. This is no time to be modest. If you don't realize how good you are, you won't enthusiastically market yourself. If you aren't enthusiastic about you, the product, how can you expect anyone else to be?

You may find yourself resisting this idea because it seems too elementary. It is elementary, but so is all detective work. Most of the work you do in Part One is detective work. You study everything about yourself, including the obvious, to find marketing advantages that you may not know you have.

As you do the detective work in Part One, you are looking at yourself as though you were someone else. Analyzing your assets will help you define you, the product. All of your assets, in themselves, don't matter. How you use them matters. The assets are what help you do what you do. Not all the assets you list will be important in the market that you choose, but some of them will make you the perfect choice for your market. That's the beauty of this process.

You have eight different kinds of assets:

1)   SKILLS
2)   PEOPLE
3)   KNOWLEDGE
4)   EXPERIENCE
5)   PERSONALITY
6)   VALUES
7)   PHYSICAL ATTRIBUTES
8)   ACCOMPLISHMENTS

First, list your skills assets.

Make a list of everything that you do well. Are you a good singer? speaker? writer? listener? organizer? manager? gardener? cook? pianist? botanist? psychic? skier? surgeon? photographer? teacher? engineer? golfer? woodworker? storyteller? cook?

Over time your list will grow. Whatever you do well should be put on the list. Every single asset goes on the list because the combination of all of your assets is what makes you you.

Write down EVERYTHING. Even if it is a skill you are not using now it is still a skill you possess. You never forget how to ride a bicycle. No skill is too small to put on the list, so don't dismiss any skill as "unimportant" or "useless." Being an expert skier might not look like it belongs on your list, but it could be a key to your target market.

Making your list will probably take days. It should. After all, you have taken a lifetime becoming who you are. You are incredibly talented and you probably don't even realize how talented you are. You never know until you examine yourself thoroughly just how talented you are.

Second, list your people assets.

We talk about people having a network. In fact, we all have a collection of networks. We have networks of people that we know today and networks of people that we knew in the past. Your collection of networks is as unique as you are. This gives you a tremendous marketing advantage once you know how to use your people assets.

No one else has done what you have done, worked where you have worked, traveled where you have traveled and experienced what you have experienced. There is overlap certainly, but no one anywhere in the world knows all the people that you know.

Your networks are a marketing gold mine. Every person you know can lead you into one of their networks, gaining you access to people you otherwise wouldn't meet. Harvey Mackay, author of <u>Swim with the Sharks</u>, has hypothesized that we are no more than five people away from anyone in the world. That means that we know someone who knows someone who knows someone who knows a person that we want to contact. I was dubious of this until I realized that there were just two people between me and the President of the United States.

A friend's daughter worked as a summer intern for a senior United States senator. Of course, the Senator knew the President. So, the chain was me … friend's daughter … senator … president. To be realistic, I would probably have to add one more person to the chain, the director of interns in the Senator's office. The chain was then me … friend's daughter … director of interns … senator … president. I can't imagine when I would try to contact the former President, but there are countless three or four or five people chains that can introduce you to the people you want to meet. The people you know truly are a marketing gold mine.

To compile your list of people assets, list all of your networks, past and present.

List your school networks: nursery school, grade school, middle school, high school.

List your college networks: dorms, sports, fraternity/sorority, clubs, honor societies, student government, service organizations.

List your neighborhood networks: current neighbors, former neighbors.

List your friend networks: friends you are in contact with frequently, friends you are in contact with infrequently.

List your work networks: co-workers, former co-workers, bosses, former bosses, clients, former clients, vendors, former vendors.

List your community service networks.

List your sports networks.

List your hobby networks.

List your personal vendor network.

List your children's networks.

(Do this even if your children are young. I know a trainer who got a contract through another parent she met at a children's birthday party at a pizza restaurant.)

List your parents' networks.

List your in-laws' networks.

List your siblings' networks.

List other relatives' networks.

As you do this exercise, list as many people as you can in each of the networks. Keep the lists handy. Add to them until you can't think of another name. Then, let your subconscious take over and remember more names while you're thinking about other things.

The rule of thumb is that each person knows 250 other people. You probably know more than 250 people. So do each of the people in each of your networks. This is why your networks are so important.

Third, list your knowledge assets.

Your list of knowledge assets includes both your education and the theoretical and practical knowledge you possess.

Education includes:

> College degrees
> Professional certifications
> Professional licenses
> Seminars/workshops
> Continuing education courses
> On-the-job training

Theoretical knowledge is what you know. Knowing the name of the last Czar of Russia or how an internal combustion engine works is theoretical knowledge.

Practical knowledge is what you know how to do. Knowing how to play a saxophone or digitally restore a damaged photograph is practical knowledge.

List all of your knowledge assets. Then, let your subconscious keep adding to your list. Something you know or something you know how to do could be the key to your target market.

Fourth, list your experience assets.

The combination of your work and life experiences is unique to you. Your experience can open doors for you that may not even have considered. For example, having been a librarian might make you an excellent author of children's books.

Your work experience includes:

A. Jobs, both paying and non-paying
B. Internships
C. Volunteer work

For each experience, list the skills that were required. You will probably be surprised at the number of different skills that you needed in each job. The combination of your skills makes you unique. No one else in the world has the same set of skills acquired in the same ways.

Your life experience includes:

A.   Family relationships
B.   Personal relationships
C.   Hobbies
D.   Travel

No one else has had the same experiences that you have had. Your history is unique to you.

Fifth, list your personality assets.

Personality assets are important because people do business with people they like.

To identify your personality assets, answer these questions:

How would you describe yourself?
Are you extroverted? introverted? creative? organized? patient? enthusiastic? loyal? funny? spontaneous? focused? hardworking? emotional? persistent? easygoing? determined? confident?
How would your family describe you?
How would your friends describe you?
How would your employers describe you?
How would your employees describe you?
How would your co-workers describe you?
How would vendors describe you?
How would your neighbors describe you?
The views of all of these people taken together complete the picture of you. Their views might not always be flattering, but remember that what one person considers a liability another person could consider an asset. Someone might describe you as "weird." However, what one person considers "weird" other people might see as "creative." One person might label you "obsessive," but other people would simply say you are "thorough." The important thing is to list all of your personality assets.

Sixth, list your values assets.

Value assets are important because people do business with people who think like they think.

What are the non-negotiables in your life? What are the things that you won't do? Murder, lie, cheat, steal, laugh at someone's failings? We all have certain beliefs about what is right and what is wrong, what we will do and what we won't do. They are so much a part of the fiber of our being that we don't even have to think about them. If you would never steal, you don't have to think about it when an opportunity presents itself. These non-negotiables reflect your values. Understanding your values is important because it would be a terrible mistake to go into a market where you would be asked to compromise those values.

Seventh, list your physical attributes.

Physical attributes are important because people do business with people who look like them and sound like them.

What do you look like? List your:

Age
Sex
Height
Weight
Hair color
Eye color
Race
Physical conditions/problems/disabilities

Eighth, list your action assets.

Action assets are the actions you took that helped clients. To make this list, start with the most recent problem you solved for a client. Going in reverse order, list the major problems you have solved in your career. Quantify your results. State them in terms of dollars and percentages. For example, if you developed a new manufacturing process that cut production time and saved money, your description of the results should tell how much production time was cut and how many dollars were saved.

For each problem, answer the following questions.

> What was the problem?
> What steps did I take to solve the problem?
> What results did I achieve?
> How long did it take me to achieve those results?

The answers to these questions will provide you with a list of your action assets. Your action assets are vitally important to your marketing efforts. You will market yourself on the basis of what you have done in the past. Past success gives credibility to what you say you will do. It is proof that you can do what you say you can do.

You are the sum total of your assets in all eight of these areas: skills, people, knowledge, experience, personality, values, physical attributes and accomplishments. You and only you have your combination of assets.

When you define yourself by your unique combination of assets, there can't be any competition. How could there be? You are unique. No one else in the world can offer exactly what you offer. This gives you an unassailable marketing advantage. The problem is that most of us don't know how to use our advantage.

Imagine an old movie, a Western. Picture the cavalry hiding behind overturned wagons while they fire nearly empty revolvers at 2,000 charging Indians. The revolvers have limited range. Pretty soon they will be empty. The soldiers are praying for someone to save them.

What they don't realize is that they have been sitting on the help that they so desperately need. There are Gatling guns in the trunks they are hiding behind. These Gatling guns would make a sizable impression on the Indians. The sad fact is that, even if they knew they had the guns, they wouldn't know how to load and fire them. Similarly, most of us already have all the weapons we need in the marketing battle. We just don't know we have them or don't know how to use them.

A friend, Michael Mattie, said something once that knocked my mental socks off. He said, "We spend a good part of our lives trying to be better than other people. All we have to do is be different from other people." Different from, not better than.

It is this difference that makes us marketable. Each of us is uniquely suited to a specific market. When a company markets a product, they start by looking for the USP, which is defined as the Unique Selling Proposition. This is what makes the product desirable to the buyer. For example, when I buy a car my foremost concern is safety so the car I buy has to have a high safety rating. For me, that is its USP. To translate USP from marketing products to marketing a person, think of USP as short for Uniquely Special Person. You are special. No one else could possibly ever be just like you and possess the collection of personal assets that you possess. That's the beauty of USP. All you have to do is find yours and market it.

To find your USP, go back to the analysis you did of yourself. Ask, "What am I good at?" Then, for each of the things, ask another question. "How can I help other people when I use this skill?" If you are creative, how could you use that skill? If you are a gourmet cook, how could you use that skill? If you are analytical, how could you use that skill?

How you use your assets to help people provides the key to your marketing strategy. The way you use your assets are the benefits that your clients get from working with you. When you market yourself, stress the benefits that you offer, not the features of your service.

What would you think if you received a brochure from a law firm that said, "We have been in business 28 years. We have twelve lawyers representing clients in seven counties. We are the largest personal injury law firm in the state?" I bet your reaction would be, "So what?"

Compare that marketing statement with this one. "In 28 years we have represented 5,000 people. Ninety-five percent of our clients have received a favorable settlement of their case. We have collected millions of dollars for our clients."

Which law firm would you call? If they aren't singing your song, you won't listen long. My song, your song, everyone's song is WIIFM, "What's in it for me?" Having a 95% chance of receiving compensation for your injuries is "WIIFM."

When a client buys your services, he is, in essence, buying you and what you are going to do for him. He is buying the benefits that you bring to him. Only you can do what you can do in the way you can do it. Only you can offer a particular package of benefits in a particular way. Your USP is your marketing advantage. It is an unbeatable advantage, if you know how to use it. By the time you finish TDS you will be using it—brilliantly.

CHAPTER TWO

FINDING YOUR MARKET

Part II of TDS, the Top Dog System, is Finding Your Market or, in Top Dog language, *Barking Up the Right Tree*. Now that you have a unique product to sell, the next step is to find a market of prospects for whom you are the perfect product. You are looking for the best market for you. The operative words are "for you." To see what I mean, think "marriage." Think of all the spouses of your happily-married friends, neighbors and co-workers. Generally, they are perfectly lovely people, but not your cup of tea. You like them, but would never want to be married to them. Yet, they are obviously the right choice for their significant other.

Similarly, there is a target market for which you are perfectly matched and other markets for which you aren't. Don't worry about this week's "hot market" or the market your presumed competitors are in or the market that your sales manager is pushing. Find the best market for you.

In my experience, the concept of succeeding by limiting ourselves is often a stumbling block. It goes against our natural instinct. One of the hardest things for people to do when they market their business is to limit themselves to one or two target markets. They think that limiting themselves reduces their opportunities. They want to sell to EVERYONE! After all, if you try to sell to everyone, some day someone will buy. Right? Right, but..... You can get mighty hungry waiting for some day. You can't be a success selling, eventually, to someone. You have to sell consistently to x number of people and generate y income in z time in order to succeed.

Although it seems safe to try to sell to everyone, it is actually an enormous marketing error. Eighty percent of the average salesperson's time is spent talking to poorly-qualified prospects. On the other hand, if you target a niche market, you spend 100% of your time, energy and money talking to highly-qualified prospects. You use your time, energy and money where you have the greatest chance of creating a return on your investment.

With a niche market, you can become an expert on them, on what they want, what they need, what they fear. You can crawl inside their skins and walk in their shoes. You know the right questions to ask them. You know the right solutions to offer them. You know what they buy. You know why they buy. You know when they buy. You know how they buy.

With a niche market you get a pool of people with shared interests and needs, with money to pay for your services, with a shared network where you can quickly build your reputation as the expert. Your reputation spreads more quickly in a small, homogeneous group. You increase your chance for referrals because clients and prospects feel safe referring you to other people in their network. You can do business every day instead of waiting for "someday."

Our natural inclination, though, is to view limiting ourselves to one target market as career suicide. Experience shows that the contrary is true. Going narrow and deep beats wide and shallow every time. It is the difference between the concentrated beam of a spotlight and the diffuse glow of a light bulb. If you go narrow and deep, you can penetrate and capture a market, becoming the provider for the market. The specialist is always successful.

Be a detective. Study your list of assets. Is there anything in your background, your education, your experience, your networks, that could give you an "in?" Do you have access to a professional group? an educational group? a group of business owners? an ethnic group? a religious group? a women's group? a men's group? a hobby group? a community service group?

Sometimes you don't even have to actively search to find potential target markets. You just have to keep your eyes and ears open. I am reminded of a segment in a former children's television program. 3-2-1 Contact™ was the third-longest-running series ever produced by the Children's Television Workshop (as it was then called). 3-2-1 Contact™ included a detective series called "The Bloodhound Gang." The gang consisted of children. They solved crimes by using their eyes and their ears, noticing what other people did not notice, hearing what other people did not hear and, then, putting together the pieces of the puzzle.

Doing market research to find a target market sometimes consists of nothing more than being observant. In one week, I read two newspaper articles that pointed to the same target market and, also, supplied the wedge to open the door to that market.

First was a story from The Associated Press. It opened with the line, "A lot of people are saving more for retirement, except baby boomers." It pointed out that the "average savings of the baby boom generation … fell 10.6% percent...."

The same information appeared in another article in a different newspaper. Baby boomers who weren't aware before that they might have a problem were aware after they read these articles. These articles alerted a potential market to a serious problem and lent legitimacy to the presentations of financial consultants who contacted this market about this problem.

> MARKET + PROBLEM + AWARENESS = OPPORTUNITY

If you find a market with a problem you can solve, you have an opportunity. If the market knows it has the problem, you have a golden opportunity. When you show them that you are the solution to the problem, doors will open.

SETTING THE CRITERIA FOR YOUR TARGET MARKET

There is a target market for which you are the best choice. You are the best choice when your assets fill the market's needs perfectly. How do you find that market?

To find it, the first thing you have to do is select the criteria you will use in choosing it. Again, it's like marriage. Choosing a target market is equivalent to choosing the type of person you want to marry.

I can hear you saying, "I don't need to do this. I'm not just starting out. I have a target market." Maybe, but, is it the best market for you?

Whether you are a new salesperson or an established salesperson, to find the best market for you, use the following six-step process.

THE PROCESS FOR FINDING A TARGET MARKET

Step one: Select the criteria you will use in choosing your target market.

Make a list of the criteria you will use in selecting your target market. This is similar to the first step you take when you buy a house. You make a list of the features you want the house to have.

The list of your criteria for the house might look like this:

* 4,000 to 5,000 square feet
* four bedrooms
* four bathrooms
* a screened-in porch
* 100 acres of land
* three-car garage
* cost no more than *x* dollars
* available on *y* date
* assumable mortgage

You also should make a list of the criteria that you don't want the house to have. Perhaps your "Do Not Want" list would look like this:

* not a split-level
* no pool or pond
* not near the airport

It is just as important that you don't get what you don't want as that you do get what you do want.

Now list the criteria for your target market. The list of your criteria for a target market might look like this:

* little competition
* homogeneous
* needs what you offer
* big enough to support you
* willing and able to pay for what you do
* market where you have experience
* market where you know the influencers

* market you like
* market with future value
* market with referral value

Will you find either a house or a target market that is perfect, i.e. that meets all of your criteria? No. That's why this is just the first step in the process. Next you have to decide which of the criteria you listed are most important. Which are "must-haves" and which are "want-to-haves?"

Step Two: Rank your criteria in order of importance.

Which of your criteria is most important to you? Which criteria are least important?

In a house perhaps cost is the most important criteria and location the second most important. Maybe least important are the 100 acres and the assumable mortgage. In beginning to look for a house you would rank all of your criteria in order of importance so that you could measure the houses you are looking at against your criteria.

Similarly, when you are choosing your target market you need to rank your criteria in order of importance. What are your "must-haves?" What are your "want-to-haves?" Perhaps money is the most important criteria. It usually is because a market that doesn't have the money to buy your services isn't a market. Period. Even if individual prospects have money, if there aren't enough of them in the market, the market won't generate the annual revenue you need and you will starve.

The criteria I chose for my market, ranked in order of importance, look like this:

1) Big enough to support me
2) Willing and able to pay
3) Needs what I offer
4) Market where I have experience
5) Market I like
6) Homogeneous market
7) Market where I know the influencers
8) Market with referral value
9) Market with future value
10) Market with little competition

The criteria on your list may be different than the criteria on my list. Even if your criteria are the same as mine, the ranking of your criteria may be different. There is no one right answer. The important thing is to know what characteristics you want a target market to have and which of those characteristics are most important to you. Having this list helps you to be objective as you go through the process of selecting a market. Just because you like a market doesn't mean it can support you. On the other hand, just because it can support you doesn't mean you would like working with it. Even if it is a viable market it may not be the market for you.

A word of advice: If you aren't excited about the prospect of working with a particular market, don't choose it no matter how well it fits your other criteria. A client slammed down the phone and greeted me with an exasperated, "I HATE doctors. They are arrogant and impossible." Guess what his target market was? Right. Doctors. Because your sales manager thinks a group is a "hot market" doesn't mean it's the right market for you. If you don't like them, don't court them. For this man, "not doctors" should have been on his "Do Not Want" list.

DETOUR for WELL-ESTABLISHED SALESPEOPLE:

If you are a well-established salesperson, before we go on to the third step, let's take a detour to see if you do, indeed, already have a target market. Start by creating a profile of your best clients, the clients that produced the most revenue for you. Ask yourself:

What are the characteristics of my top twenty clients?
Do they all have the same characteristics?
Who are they? Are they all retired schoolteachers or senior executives in transportation companies or women owners of manufacturing businesses?
Do I know where to find a big pool of prospects that match the profile of my top clients?

If your top clients have a similar profile, if your other clients share that profile, if you have an ample prospect pool that matches the profile, you do indeed have a target market and can skip the rest of this chapter. If the only thing your clients have in common is the fact that they are your clients, you don't have a target market. You have good luck. How long is your luck going to hold? When it runs out, you'll need to find a target market that is right for you and one that will produce greater revenue with less effort. So, on to Step Three.

Step Three: Find specific markets that meet your criteria.

Once you have selected and ranked your criteria, you need to find specific markets that match your criteria. To find these possible markets, ask yourself:

Who could benefit from what I do?
How large is this potential market?
Is it large enough to support me?
What experience do I have with this market?
What are the needs of this market?
What services already exist to meet these needs?
Could I provide these services in a better way?
Could I provide a better service?

To create a profile of the best target market for you, list all the people who could benefit from your services. Break this list into clusters of people using demographics and psychographics. Demographics are factual information. Psyhographics are psychological information. Demographics tell you who people are. Psychographics tell you what people want and what they like.

To see how this works, let's choose a mythical prospect named Karl Chevette. Demographic information would tell you that Karl Chevette is 62 years old, married, has two children, owns a home at 14 Classic St., Rutland, Vt. and is a computer graphic artist at Classic Cars. Psychographic information would tell you that Mr. Chevette is a car buff who loves rallying. It would also tell you that he likes jazz and Ben and Jerry's ice cream.

After you group your prospects into clusters using demographics and psychographics make a profile of your potential markets. You will want to set a geographical boundary. The size of the boundary is determined by the nature of your business. For example, a market could be all dental hygienists in New York State or all brides in your metropolitan area or all fly-fishermen in the Pacific Northwest. If your market is computer graphic artists in the Northeast, Mr. Chevette could fit your profile.

Be careful when you define potential markets. A demographic group is not necessarily a market. It may be far too large and diverse. For example, there is no such thing as a women's market or a men's market. Instead, there are a variety of different markets composed of women and a variety of different markets comprised of men.

Women are not a target market. Affluent women who are grandmothers are a target market. Women who own printing companies are a market. Women rabbis are a market.

As you break down large demographic groups into clusters or smaller groups with similar characteristics, you are segmenting the market. Each of these clusters is a niche or segment. That's why you will hear the term "niche marketing" or "segment marketing" used inter-changeably with "target marketing." It doesn't matter what you call it. It matters that you do it.

For example, you could break the category of women down into many different segments. You may want to work with women under 60. That's a segment. Then, you could divide that segment, or piece of the pie, into women under 60 who own businesses. That's a smaller segment or micro-segment. Then, you could divide that micro-segment again. You could divide it into women under 60 who own janitorial services.

Then, you might want to ask yourself, "Am I using the best criteria to define my market? Why choose women under 60? Why not just use the broader criteria of women who own janitorial services?" That could be the micro-segment you end up targeting. If that micro-segment is too narrow, meaning there are too few women who meet those criteria in your city and you have to limit yourself geographically, you could increase the size of the micro-segment by defining it as all women who own service businesses in your city.

If that's too big a market, you could target women in your city who own service businesses that employ less than 100 people. You can keep adjusting the criteria until you come up with a target market that is big enough to support you. When you finish segmenting, you might end up with a target market of women in your city who own service businesses that employ 50 to 100 people.

Step Four: Rate each possible market chosen in Step Three.

Use the list of ten criteria that you chose in Step One. If a potential market meets the most important criteria on your list, give it ten points. If it meets the second most important criteria, give it nine points. If it meets the third most important criteria on your list, give it eight points and so on. If a target market met all of the criteria on your list, it would get 55 points. Do the math for each of your possible markets. Then, based on the total number of points each market received, rank the markets in order of how well they met the criteria that are important to you.

Step Five: From your list of possible markets, select the best target market for you.

It might be the market that got the most number of points, but it might not be. There is no point in spending what could be many years working with clients that you don't like. Choose a market that truly appeals to you. Does the thought of working with the people in a certain market excite you or does it create a knot in your stomach? In this step, choose a market that you want to work with. Listen to your gut. Don't be like my client who targeted doctors because his sales manager wanted him to and hated every minute working with them. If the market that received the most number of points is a market that you don't want to work with, don't.

You are, literally, marrying this target market. You don't want to have to go through a divorce and start over. Does this look like a good marriage? Ask yourself, "Do I like this group of people enough to marry them?" They may be a wonderful market, but, if you don't like them, you will be miserable and do miserably. A market is like a spouse. He or she may be "perfect," but not for you.

Before you make your final decision, listen to your gut. Does your gut tell you the market you are choosing is the best choice for you? Which markets do you think would be the most fun, not just the most profitable? Profit is great, but profit and fun together are fantastic.

Does your gut tell you to choose one of the other markets even if it scored fewer points? If so, go with your gut. It's never wrong. The head is often wrong. The heart is sometimes wrong. The gut is never wrong. Unfortunately for us, the gut is easy to ignore.

CHAPTER THREE

GETTING TO KNOW YOUR MARKET

Now you are ready for Part Three of TDS, the Top Dog System. Part Three is Getting to Know Your Market or, in Top Dog terms, *Studying their Pedigrees*. Before you hire someone, you read their resume, interview them and do a background check. You need to follow the same procedure when you select your target market. You want to know your prospects bone-deep. Crawl into their heads and hearts. Walk in their shoes. Get to know them from the inside out. Your strategy is to find out everything you can about them and use what you find to penetrate the market.

Study the demographic profile of your market. Who are your prospects? Are they women under sixty who own service businesses in your county or female senior executives in manufacturing companies in the Northeast or affluent first-time mothers who live in the NYC area?

Study the psychographic profile of your prospects. Are they golfers who are retired, like classical music, vote Republican, travel, and drive BMW's or outdoor sportsmen who like to fish and hunt, drive a pick-up truck and listen to country music?

Studying your market reminds me of the lyrics from the song, "Getting to Know You," in the movie, THE KING AND I.

Getting to know you.
Getting to know all about you.
Getting to like you.
Getting to hope you like me.

After you study the demographic and psychographic profiles, become a detective and build a psychological profile. The psychological profile tells you who they are inside. To do this you have to get into their heads. Read what they write. Read what they read. Read what is written about them. What do they want? What do they fear? What would lead them to call you? What would prevent them from calling you? What problems do they have? What solutions can you offer?

The most important question is, "What do they fear?" Pain and pleasure are the two driving forces in life. We do things either to get pleasure or to avoid pain and we will do more to avoid pain than we will to get pleasure. What pain does your target market want to avoid? You can't sell someone if you don't know what he wants and what he fears.

I call the answers to these questions customer intelligence.

CUSTOMER INTELLIGENCE

How do you learn about your target market? There are three ways. First, go to the popular and/or business press to see what is being written about your prospects and their hopes and fears. Read what other people say about them in newspapers and magazines and books. Read everything written about them in the past two years. Second, read what they say about themselves and about the things that are important to them. Third, ask them. You can do this individually or by asking groups of people in a seminar. It is a terrible waste of time and money and effort to try to "solve" problems they don't have while being unaware of problems they do have or to offer to solve minor problems and ignore major problems.

If you can't find "them" written about, you don't have a "them." Your market is too broad and will have to be segmented more narrowly. That would be disappointing news, but it is actually excellent information to acquire now before you waste time, money and effort trying to sell to a market that doesn't exist.

After you find the answers to what your customers want and what they fear, you need to know if they feel the competition is meeting their needs. Is someone else helping them get what they want or are your competitors failing to meet their expectations? I call this information competitor intelligence.

COMPETITOR INTELLIGENCE

Competitor intelligence is the business equivalent of military intelligence. Who are your competitors? Where are they? Who is serving your target market? How are they reaching them? What are they saying to them? You could find out by asking your prospects what they like about their current service provider and what they dislike. What do they wish their current provider did? What do they wish he didn't do?

Competitor intelligence helps you find out what your competition is doing and find a way to do it better. Ask what your target market doesn't like about doing business with your competitors and what it wishes your competitors did more of or less of or did better. Ask yourself if you can do something your competitors don't do or can do something that they do better than they do it. If you are strong in areas where your competition is weak, you have a marketing advantage.

If you are unique, why do you need competitor intelligence? You need it because you are always looking for a wedge to open the prospect's door. That wedge may be dissatisfaction with their current service provider.

A word of caution: As you ask questions about your competitors, be careful to not make negative comments about your competition. After all, the prospect chose to do business with them. It is a delicate balancing act to find out where your competition is weak without making the prospect feel that he made a mistake.

Used together customer and competitor intelligence help you find a door into your market. Customer intelligence tells you what your prospects want and what they fear. Competitor intelligence tells you where your competitors are falling short of meeting your prospects' expectations. Their failings are your opportunities.

Do you want to take these opportunities? After you have created a profile of your market and done customer and competitor intelligence, ask yourself, "Is this still the market I want to go after?" If not, go back to your list of potential target markets. Take your second choice and study it as thoroughly as you studied this market. It's better to call off the wedding before than to divorce later.

CHATER FOUR

INTRODUCING YOURSELF
TO YOUR MARKET

Once you have chosen the target market that is best for you, you are ready for Part Four, Introducing Yourself to Your Market aka *Barking up a Storm*. To do this, you will need a marketing plan. Remember, the goal of TDS, the Top Dog System, is to have prospects call you and ask to do business with you. They can't do that if they don't know you exist and they won't know you exist unless you tell them.

The marketing plan is nothing more than a strategy to reach and sell to the market you have chosen. You can be the best whatever in the world and know exactly who would benefit from your services, but you can't sell them unless you can get access to them and make them want you. To do this, you have to package your product so that it will appeal to your market. Then, you have to capitalize on this appeal, creating a desire in the market for you, the product.

Every product needs to be packaged. In order to create the most appealing package, a manufacturing company studies the product's specifications. They ask, "What is it? How is it made? What does it do? What can't it do? What are its strengths? What are its weaknesses?" You have to ask these same questions about yourself and your services. "What can you do? How do you do it? What are your strengths? What are your weaknesses? What can't you do?"

The goal of packaging is to make the product appealing to the market. To do this, the package has to say, "Here I am. I am the best solution to your problem."

Packaging is what makes you recognizable. Packaging is what helps people remember you. To be successful you have to be the person who snaps into sharp focus in the prospect's mind, just as the scene in the camera's viewfinder snaps into focus when you turn the focusing ring. You have to build an identity that is unique so that your prospects recognize and remember you. Everything you do and everything you say has to send the same message. Quaker Oats doesn't change their packaging for Old-fashioned Oats every day. You shouldn't change your packaging, either.

Your package should be designed so that it highlights specific assets. Your package is the message that you send to your market. You have to deliver one consistent message. Everything you do and everything you say has to send that message. Packaging is nothing more than taking the collection of amazing assets that you identified in Part One, selecting the assets that will appeal to the specific market that you selected in Parts Two and Three and putting the assets into a distinct, easily-recognized package.

This is where many people make a huge marketing error. Many people actually sabotage their marketing efforts. They dilute their marketing advantage by not creating distinctive packaging. They identify themselves the same way everyone else does. They use generic packaging so that they look like and sound like everyone else. Do you remember when generic products first came on the market and were packaged in white boxes with black lettering? Every product was packaged the same as every other product. Every product looked like every other product. Don't be a me-too, generic, white box.

WRITING YOUR IDENTITY STATEMENT

How you describe yourself to other people is your packaging. The rule used to be that we all needed a two-minute identity statement to describe ourselves. Then, the rule changed to a thirty-second identity statement. But whether your statement takes two minutes to say or only thirty seconds, it is amazing the damage that a poorly-constructed identity statement can do to your marketing. By the time you have introduced yourself, not only can't I figure out what you do, but I see no reason to stick around to try to figure it out.

To make sure this never happens to you instead of a thirty-second identity statement write an identity statement that has no more than four words. An example would be, "I am a marketing coach." It has to tell clearly what you do. Other examples are: "I am an accountant." "I am a NASCAR driver." "I am a pediatric neurosurgeon." "I am the executive director of The Urban League." The identity statement says, "This is what I am." It says it so clearly that every listener will understand.

Coming up with a four-word-or-less identity statement isn't easy. When I started, I had trouble coming up with less than fourteen words.

Exercise: Write your own four-word identity statement.

"I am a _____ _____ _____ _____."

WRITING YOUR ACTION STATEMENT

Once you can say what you are in four words or less, create a one-sentence action statement that tells people what you do and for whom you do it. The action statement says "I do _____ for _____" or "I help _____ to _____."

> I train dolphins for Ocean World.
> I repair umbilical hernias in infants.
> I help business owners secure lines of credit.

My identity statement is, "I am a marketing coach." My action statement is, "I help professional service providers increase their income." If I were a physical therapist, my four-word identity statement would be "I am a physical therapist." My action statement could be "I help people learn to walk again after brain injury."

CREATING YOUR PERSONAL MARKETING STATEMENT

When you combine your identity statement and your action statement you create your personal marketing statement. Your personal marketing statement is your packaging. It tells everyone you meet, and the 250 people they each know, what you do and whom you help.

People want to know who you are and what you do. Whatever they are buying, your market always has one concern: WIIFM, "What's in it for me?" Your packaging answers that question. It tells them why they would want you and, equally important, why their friends and colleagues would want you.

A common marketing mistake people make is to give the wrong answer to the question, "What do you do?" When people ask a person what he does, he usually answers by telling them what he is. If you are a financial consultant and I ask you what do you do, you would probably say, "I'm a financial consultant". That's not what you do. That's what you are. What do you do? If your target market is women business owners, your answer could be, "I help women business owners build a personal nest egg." That's what you do.

If you simply tell them what you are, they can assume that they don't need your services and stop listening. I heard about a wonderful strategy that one person uses to keep himself from being bothered by other passengers on an airplane. If the person sitting next to him asks him what he does, he replies, "I sell life insurance." End of conversation. You don't want your conversations to end before they begin.

When you tell them what you do, be sure not to also tell them how you do it. If you say, "I help women business owners build a personal nest egg by investing in tax-sheltered annuities" you are telling your listener too much.

An excellent way to use your personal marketing statement is a technique I learned when I attended a seminar led by Paul and Sarah Edwards, bestselling authors of numerous books including <u>Finding Your Perfect Work</u>. They recommended that you answer the question, "What do you do?" with another question that begins with the words, "Do you know how....?" Their example was, "Do you know how some people don't go to the dentist because they are afraid?" After the person replied that he knew people who didn't go to the dentist because of fear, the dentist would say, "Well, I specialize in treating people who are afraid to go to a dentist." You notice, the dentist doesn't tell how he treats those people. He just says that he specializes in treating them.

When you meet someone, you want to make sure you have his attention before you begin to market yourself. Asking him a question is a guaranteed way to get his attention. For example, if you are an orthopedic surgeon you could ask, "Do you know how some people have pain in their knees and have trouble getting out of a chair?" Then you wait for a sign that the person knows what you are talking about. He may answer, "I'm one of those people." If he does, you have his attention.

You need to get the listener to identify with the pain. People will do more to get away from pain than they will to get to pleasure. You want to package yourself so that people will know that they or someone they know needs what you do. When the listener realizes he or someone he knows needs your services, the conversation will continue rather than ending before you have "hooked" your listener.

Everyone you meet has the potential to market you. Whether or not they do depends on your packaging. Great packaging allows you to create a strong, ongoing, business-generating machine. By giving everyone you meet the information they need to become your marketing department, you leverage your time and energy and money

People can't market you if they don't know you exist.
People can't market you if they don't know what you do.
People can't market you if they don't know for whom you do it.

My insurance agent got my business because someone else marketed him. I was very unhappy with my long-time agent. Another agent who prospected me about homeowners insurance did not sell business insurance, but he knew someone who did and asked if that person could call me. I am positively delighted with my new insurance agent, Mike, but I would never have found him if someone else had not marketed him. The other agent could not have marketed Mike if Mike hadn't packaged himself well. Mike gave the other agent the information he needed to market him. The other agent understood what Mike did and who would be a good client for Mike.

SELLING THE PACKAGE

The packaging gets the product noticed. The packaging may get the product bought. What is your packaging? Your packaging is your personal marketing statement. The best personal marketing statement meets the same four criteria that the best product packaging meets.

> Packaging must be clear, concise, compelling and consistent.

First, your packaging, i.e. your personal marketing statement, must be clear. "I specialize in helping women business owners build personal net eggs" is clear because it uses layman's terminology, not a financial professional's terminology.

Second, your marketing statement must be concise. I was sitting in a meeting where each person had been asked to stand up and introduce himself. We were allotted thirty seconds for our introductions. When one man finished his four-minute "30-second" introduction, the man sitting on my left leaned over and asked, "Do you have any idea what he just said?"

I certainly didn't. I was sure that no one else in the room did, either. Four-Minute-Man lost an opportunity to market himself. He lost the chance to market himself to not only the forty people who were in the room, but also to the 250 people that each of us knew and the 250 people that each of those people knew.

How many people do you know? It could well be more than 250. How many of those people understand exactly what you do? Not kind of what you do or where you work, but exactly what you do?

Third, your personal marketing statement must be compelling. If your marketing statement says you can solve a problem that the listener has or someone he knows has, your statement will be compelling. If it is, you increase the chances that he will remember you. If you are an eye doctor who specializes in laser surgery for cataracts and the listener's grandmother has cataracts, your statement, "I am an ophthalmologist who specializes in cataract surgery," is compelling.

Fourth, your marketing statement must be consistent. A personal marketing statement that is clear, concise and compelling is useless unless it is consistent. You have to introduce yourself the exact same way every single time. The more exposures a prospect has to you the greater the chance that he will recognize and remember you. Only if he remembers you and understands clearly what you do can he promote you. Package yourself the same way every time.

If you have your personal marketing statement ready and use it consistently, everyone you meet will know what you do and who your target market is. Your marketing statement should be so ingrained that someone could wake you up at 2 a.m. and you could repeat it.

Every single time you introduce yourself introduce yourself the same way. You can do several things exceedingly well, but nobody can remember several things. If we are lucky, people will remember one thing about us and tell other people.

The truth of this was brought home to me a few months ago. I had a luncheon meeting. We were discussing a seminar that I was going to do for an organization of women business owners. As I was preparing to leave, I heard a man's voice. I hadn't heard him or anyone else seated around us the entire time we were in the restaurant. He said to the man sitting across from him, "You have to sell me so that I can sell you to other people." I couldn't have said it better myself.

Sell yourself well so that others can sell you. In order to do this, you will need to define yourself in a way that is clear, concise, consistent and compelling. Someone you meet today could become part of your marketing department, but only if he understands who you are, what you do and for whom you do it.

TAKING YOURSELF TO MARKET

Once you have a compelling, concise, comprehensible personal marketing statement that you use consistently, you have packaged yourself well. Now you have the same problem a box of corn flakes has. How do you get someone to buy you and take you home? Just because you are sitting on the shelf in the store where your target market shops doesn't mean they will want you. How do you get them to choose you instead of everyone else who does what you do? Do you remember the old adage, "A girl chases a guy until he catches her." How do you induce prospects to chase you until you catch them? Remember, the ultimate goal of Top Dog Marketing is to have your prospects call you and ask to do business with you.

Before someone will buy you, three things have to happen. First, they have to know you. This is visibility. Second, they have to believe you. This is credibility. Third, they have to want you. This is desirability. The need for visibility and credibility cannot be overestimated. Without them, no one will ever buy you.

There are five basic ways to build visibility, credibility and desirability. First, have your prospects read what you write. Second, have them see you. Third, have them hear you. Fourth, have them read about you. Fifth, have them hear about you. That is marketing in its simplest terms. Read you. See you. Hear you. Read about you. Hear about you. That's Marketing 101.

To create visibility, you should constantly look for venues where your target market can see you, hear you, read your words, hear about you and read about you. Furthermore, you need to do this in the time you have available, within the budget you have and in a way that plays to your strengths. Then, you need to do it again and again and again. Be involved in the same professional associations as your target market. Speak at their meetings. Write for their newsletters. Do seminars for their members. Volunteer for the program committee or the membership committee.

You are better suited for some of these activities than you are for others. Study yourself and play to your strengths. If you aren't comfortable speaking, you can still do seminars. Instead of being the presenter, have the outside product expert do the presentation while you simply welcome the audience, introduce the speaker and close the program.

As you do these things you become visible. The more visible you are, the more credible you become. When you are interviewed and when you are published, people believe that you are extremely knowledgeable. Credibility builds desire.

Who is the most desirable person? The most desirable person is The Expert. The Expert is the person who is most-quoted, most-written-about, most-read-about, most-heard-of, most-heard-from, most-sought-after.

Your goal is to make yourself The Expert in your target market. You are marketing yourself, not the stocks you sell or the gallbladder surgery you perform or the legal advice you provide or the gardens you design. And you are marketing yourself in a very specific way—as The Expert.

To understand why this is the best way to market yourself, put yourself in your prospect's shoes. Crawl into his mind. See the world through his eyes. Why does he want to talk to you? read your letter? attend your seminar? meet with you? trust you?

He doesn't. There is nothing to propel him to start doing business with you. That's why it is so difficult to woo someone away from his current service provider. It's always easier to maintain the status quo. It seems safer to continue to do what you have been doing even if you aren't happy with the results than to do something different. It's a case of, "Better the devil you know than the one you don't."

Not only do we have to overcome inertia, but we also have to overcome the fast pace of modern life. We function in overdrive. Our to-do lists are longer than our arms. Even children are starting to live this way. I heard a four-year old boy say, "I'm so busy my to-do list has two pages." We don't have time to do what we need to do, much less time to investigate making a change. We also function in the media equivalent of a war zone. We are bombarded by thousands of media messages every day. It is impossible to attend to all of them. We can't so we don't. We tune out most of them.

Because of this, there is a high brick wall between our prospect and us. He may be looking at us and talking to us, but the wall is there. If he is having a bad day, the wall is thicker and higher. We can try to go over it or under it or around it. The easiest way, though, is to have the prospect open the door for us. That is asking a lot. We are asking the prospect to take time he doesn't have and attend to one of the thousands of messages he gets a day. We are asking him to make a change. We are asking him to trust us.

Why should he believe anything we say even if we can get him to attend to what we are saying? He shouldn't, unless someone he trusts recommends us, explicitly or implicitly. If a newspaper prints our article, it is implicitly endorsing us. If someone refers us, he is explicitly endorsing us. Either way, we need an endorsement to get past the prospect's fear. We have all had bad experiences in the past with someone with whom we've done business. We're wary.

The greatest endorsement we can have is the endorsement of being The Expert. You can become The Expert by knowing your target market. You can study them thoroughly. You can know them as well as, if not better than, they know themselves. You can be The Expert in meeting their needs.

How do they know that you are Their Expert? They don't. Not until you tell them. Snowflakes are unique, but we wouldn't know it unless we were told. No one knew it before "Snowflake" Bentley began photographing them in 1885. Your target market won't know you are the unique solution to their problems unless they are told. That is why everything you do has to paint the picture of you as The Expert.

Let's see how to select the marketing tools that will sell you to your market.

SELECTING MARKETING TOOLS

What tools are available to you to build your visibility, credibility and desirability? Advertising, public relations (PR), personal marketing and direct mail marketing are marketing tools. Let's begin by eliminating advertising and direct mail marketing. These tools are fantastic if you are selling widgets, but you are selling yourself. Your primary product is not the services you sell, but you yourself. You are creating the image of yourself as Top Dog. Nobody believes you are great because you pay for a newspaper or magazine ad to tell them or pay for a delivered-to-your-door direct-mail ad.

That leaves us with PR and personal marketing. These are the tools of Top Dog Marketing. With PR, your target market believes what they read about you. You don't tell them you are great. Someone they respect tells them you are great. In personal marketing, they see you in non-work environments and tell themselves you are great.

P.T. Barnum, the great 19th century showman who joined with James Bailey to create "The Greatest Show on Earth," said, "Without publicity, a terrible thing happens. Nothing." PR has made many a career. It's why celebrities are celebrities. Celebrities have PR agents. You can, too. You can be your own PR agent. You can do the same things any PR agent does.

PR tools fall into two categories, speaking and writing.

Speaking:

1. Speeches
2. Seminars
3. Radio interviews
4. TV interviews

Writing:

1. Letters to the editor
2. Articles for magazines, newspapers, your newsletter, other people's newsletters
3. Newsletters
4. Book endorsements
5. Press kit
6. Special events

Just as you can do a seminar if you aren't a gifted speaker, you can get your name in print, even if you are not a writer. You can get someone else to take your ideas and write the draft of an article. Then, you can revise the draft or have your ghostwriter make the revisions you want.

With so many PR tools available, which of them should you choose? Choose the tools that play to your strengths and that have the greatest likelihood of reaching your audience. The following questions will help guide your choice of PR tools.

1. What am I good at?
2. What do I like to do?
3. What tools would have the greatest possibility of reaching my target market and its influencers?

If a tool will reach your market and doesn't play to your strengths, you can still use it. You won't have to eliminate any of these tools, but your own talents and the nature of your target market will dictate how big a part a specific tool plays in your marketing plan.

If you love to speak, 20% of your marketing time might be spent on writing for publication, 25% networking, 20% giving speeches and 35% doing seminars. If you love to write, 50% of your time might be spent writing for publication. The remaining time might be divided equally between doing seminars and networking. The proportion does not matter. What does matter is that you set aside a definite period of time each week for marketing, that you do indeed use that time for marketing and that you select the marketing tools that play to your strengths.

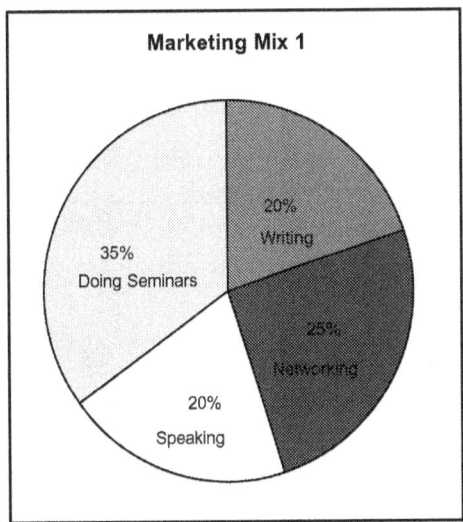

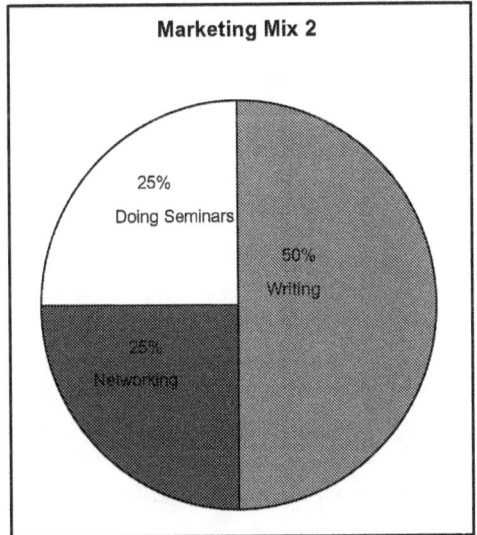

If you love to speak and your market will come to seminars, you will do more of them than someone who would rather die than speak and whose audience has neither the time nor the inclination to attend a seminar. If you are afraid of speaking in public, you are in the majority. When surveyed, over 90% of people say they would rather die than speak in public. Of course, if push came to shove, I'm sure they wouldn't want that statement to be taken literally. I am equally sure, though, that there are very few people who, like me, adore speaking and would happily speak to an audience every day, morning, noon and night. Of course, I'm helped by the fact that salespeople make the best audiences. They're enthusiastic, self-confident and fun.

As you use these PR tools, you build the perception of yourself as the expert. That doesn't mean that you will use all these tools. Rather, you will look at the range of PR tools and select the tools that best suit you and your target market. Play to your strengths with an individualized plan that builds on your strengths in areas where you will be seen and heard by your target market.

Whatever marketing tools you choose, everything you do has to be part of a total marketing campaign. You need a marketing plan, not just isolated activities. A marketing plan always has a goal. A goal might be to increase your revenue by 10% in the next year. A marketing plan also has specific action steps that you need to take to achieve your goal. An example of an action step might be to have three magazine articles submitted for publication in the next six months.

Your goal and the action steps you take to achieve it must be quantifiable and measurable and timed. They could be stated in the following terms.

My goal is to _____ by _____.

In order to reach my goal, I will do _____ by _____ and _____ by _____ and _____ by _____."

Have a plan to reach both prospects and their influencers and work the plan. The obvious influencers are lawyers and accountants, but those are just the most obvious. For example, business brokers, officers in trade associations, officers in professional associations, officers in clubs can also be influencers. Athletic trainers could be centers of influence if your market consists of amateur cyclists and obstetricians and midwives and pediatricians if your market consists of new mothers.

Work backwards from the desired result, creating a timetable for the action steps you need to take to achieve the result. Otherwise, you will have activity, but no action. Each thing you do may seem like it is just a drop in the bucket, but it takes every drop to make the bucket overflow. When it does, you have reached critical mass. Your marketing will take on a life of its own.

A necessary part of working the plan is refining it. If seminars will reach your audience, you should do seminars consistently over a long period of time, but that doesn't mean that you have to do the same seminar in the same place at the same time. Work the plan, but constantly rework the details.

INCREASING THE EFFECTIVENESS OF YOUR MARKETING

There are three critical components of a marketing plan that are often overlooked: measurement, testing and leverage. These components, if included, remarkably increase the effectiveness of your marketing.

The first component is measurement. You need to measure the effectiveness of each marketing tool. Did a specific action step yield a positive result? Did it increase sales? By how much? Did it lead to referrals? How many?

For example, when you do a seminar, you should know the answers to the following questions:

How many influencers attended the seminar?
How many prospects did I gain from the seminar?
How many of those prospects were referred by influencers?
Of the prospects I acquired, how many became clients?
How much did it cost me to get each client?
Can I modify my seminar procedure so that I spend less and still get the same or better results?

If you are writing articles, you will want to know the answers to these questions:

Which magazines yielded the best results in terms of inquiries from prospects? Which journals? Which newsletters?

When you measure, you are doing a reality check. You are asking, "Did it work? If so, how well did it work?"

The second component is testing. Testing allows you to answer questions about whether you can improve the effectiveness of your marketing. Direct mail marketers constantly test every aspect of their mailings: the headline, the body copy, the offer, the graphics, the font, the color of the paper, etc. You have to be as thorough. There is no point in doing something that is not working. There is no point in continuing to do something that is working well if you could modify it so that it works better. TEST, TEST, TEST.

If you are doing seminars, which days of the week yielded the best return on investment? What times? What locations? Which invitations? What advertisements? Which newspapers? Which headline? Which topic?

Once you have the answers to these questions, you can revise your strategy. Continuing to use a strategy that isn't working or that could work better if modified is as bad as not using a strategy at all. Time is money and time is limited.

The third component of the marketing plan that can greatly improve its effectiveness is leverage. Leverage insures that you get the most mileage out of every marketing dollar you spend and every minute you spend on marketing. To leverage your investment always make a marketing tool do double duty, at the minimum. Triple or quadruple duty is even better. The more use you get out of each marketing tool, the less it costs you.

Don't write an article in one magazine and assume you have marketed. Mail reprints of the article to prospects and clients. Include reprints in your seminar packets. Submit the article to a national publication if it was originally printed in a regional publication. Turn the article into a speech. Use it as a chapter in a book.

Your overall strategy should look like this:

Action step→ Measurement→Test → Strategy revision→Leverage

Decide on an action step. Take it. Measure its effectiveness. Then, test different modifications and change your strategy based on your test results. Finally, use leverage to get as much benefit out of each marketing action as you possibly can.

At this point you may be thinking, "There aren't enough hours in the day and I don't want to do any of those things, anyway." Of course, you could skip the whole thing. Many salespeople do choose to skip marketing or to do it in a half-hearted fashion. They take time to mail out sales literature that prospects use to line their bird cages. But, they don't take the time to market.

You don't have to market either. However, if you considered that an option, you wouldn't be reading this book. If you wanted to be a failure, you would have saved your money and time. You want to be Top Dog.

Admittedly, marketing does have drawbacks. It does take time. It does take money. It isn't easy. It can be uncomfortable. It may seem like you are bragging. You aren't. Remember when you were in second grade? When the teacher asked a question, you yelled, "I know! I know!" while you literally bounced up and down in your chair, so excited you couldn't contain yourself. You weren't being impolite. You were being enthusiastic. You were saying, "Look at me! Look at me! I know the answer. I'm the expert."

That's what marketing is. Marketing is seeing drowning men, rowing out in your rowboat and hollering, "Look at me. I can help you. Grab hold of the rope."

In truth, whatever business you are in, you are also in the marketing business. Every successful businessman is ultimately a successful marketer. In the beginning, marketing isn't a matter of success. It is a matter of survival. If you don't do it, you will have plenty of time. It takes only an hour or so a week to check in with the unemployment office. After you survive, marketing spells the difference between thriving and merely continuing to survive. It is a lot more fun and immensely more profitable to succeed, not just survive.

When a clients asks me, "How much time should I spend on marketing?" I reply, "How much time can you spend?" The more time you can spend on marketing the better. The minimum amount of time to spend is 10%, which translates to roughly one hour per day. That's the minimum.

Fortunately, once you have a marketing program in place, it works for you, even when you aren't working on it. The best marketing tactics take on a life of their own and, like the Energizer bunny, just keep going.

An article you write for magazine A can later appear in magazine B, in newsletter C and as a chapter in book D. It can be included in seminar handouts, press kits and sales literature. In fact, if you aren't leveraging each marketing activity, you aren't maximizing the return on your time and money. Top Dog didn't get on top by wasting either and neither will you. Make every marketing effort do double or triple duty. Maximize your time. Minimize your expense.

Marketing is a Catch-22 as anyone who has been in business longer than a year will tell you. When you are working at your business, you don't have time to grow your business. However, if you don't continually grow your business, you will one day have no business. If you're not growing it, it is dying, even if it looks healthy.

You need a system that combines short-term survival and long-term success. You have to have a foot in each boat—today and tomorrow—balancing what you need to do to survive today with what you need to do to succeed tomorrow.

The greater the variety of marketing tools you use, the greater the chance that you will be visible to your target market. When you start doing seminars, keep doing them on a regular basis—weekly, monthly, quarterly. It takes two years to properly evaluate a tool's effectiveness. However, don't just do seminars.

Speak, write for magazines, do community service, network. Speak to the organizations to which your target market belongs. Appear on the radio shows they listen to and the TV shows they watch. Serve on boards with them. Volunteer for the same community organizations.

Each venue increases your visibility in your target market. Visibility increases your credibility and credibility increases your prospects' level of comfort with you and level of trust in you.

Let's also remember the Top Dog truth. You can spend as much time and effort being a failure as you can being a success. Given that, as we analyze each of these tools, we will talk about what to do, why to do it, how to do it, when to do it and where to do it. In addition to that, we will talk about how to get the maximum leverage out of each marketing activity.

If you sponsor a special event, such as a fundraising dinner for the local art museum, are interviewed by a television station about the event, add the event write-up to your press kit and receive publicity about the special event in the "Events of the Week" section of your local newspaper, you have gained three extra media exposures as a result of one marketing activity, the special event.

Getting maximum leverage is critically important because exposure is the name of the game. It takes several exposures before a prospect remembers you. After that, it takes ongoing exposures in order for you to stay in the prospect's mind. Exposure equals visibility. Visibility is the baseline of marketing. If they don't see you, they don't remember you. If they don't remember you, you, essentially, don't exist. Top Dog is always visible. You must be, too.

THINK INK

The cartoon character, Ziggy, once said, "I ink. Therefore, I am." If your prospects don't read the words you write and/or read words written about you, professionally you aren't. You may work hard, but you will never be The Expert. There are no unknown, invisible experts.

Your target market and their influencers are influenced by the media. There is a commonly-held belief that what you read in the paper is true. There is another belief that people who write articles are experts. The media is a key component of any successful marketing campaign. Without the media, to quote P. T. Barnum, "a terrible thing happens. Nothing."

The value of the written word to your career is incalculable. Consequently, the first PR tool to focus on is "Getting Ink." The more times your prospects read what you have written and read what is written about you, the closer you come to being seen as The Expert. Each exposure to you builds your credibility and creates your desirability. Of course, the biggest credibility-builder is a book. Since the thought of writing a book can be daunting, it is best to start with something easier and quicker. Write an article. Once you have written several articles, you will have the building blocks for a book.

Writing for publication is not as difficult as you might think. Every day editors of magazines and journals have pages and pages to fill. Their readers want education and information. They want solutions to their problems. Your article can provide the solution. Your topic can be as simple as "Five ways to....." or "What to do when...."

> TIP: While you want to create the perception of you as the expert, you need to be careful not to appear to be trying to sell your services. Your article needs to say, "I can help you," not, "I want to sell you this."

While some publications are more prestigious than others, where you are published is nowhere near as important as the fact that you are published. Oftentimes people say to me, "I read your article in such-and-such newspaper or magazine."

The article was often in a different publication. I used to gently let them know which publication had actually published the article. One day, I realized that it didn't matter. Only five things mattered: one, it was published; two, they read it; three, they liked it; four, they remembered it; five, they remembered that I wrote it.

DECISIONS TO MAKE BEFORE YOU WRITE AN ARTICLE

As you consider writing an article for publication, there are six decisions to be made before you put pen to paper: the publication to which you are going to submit the article, the subject of the article, the angle from which you will write about the subject, the format of the article, the timing for submission of the article and the ways you plan to use the article to market yourself.

Publication + subject + angle + format + timing+ usage = marketing success.

First, decide how you will use the article to market yourself. It may seem to be putting the last step first, but it is better to know all the potential uses for an article before you write it than to try to figure them out later. Will you be able to submit it to several different magazines over a period of time or is the material time-sensitive and, therefore, able to be used for only a short period of time? Can you use the material in a newsletter? a book? a speech? a seminar?

Each article you write should help your marketing. Otherwise, there is no point in writing it. An article will do you the most good if you can use it many times. Everything you do needs to serve more than one purpose. That's leverage.

Knowing how you want to use the article in the future will help you plan the material that you want to include in the article. Articles have long legs. I was called by a prospect one snowy February afternoon. She had just returned from the Bahamas. While sitting on the beach, she read an article I had written in a business magazine. The article was in the August issue of the magazine. She said, "I wait until I go on vacation to catch up on my reading."

All of your marketing efforts, if well-done, will have long legs. I am still amazed that one afternoon I received phone calls from three people who had been given my name two years before. One didn't need my services until then, even though she was still in the same job. Another one hadn't needed my services two years before, but did then because he had changed jobs. I can't remember why the third person waited two years. My mind was screaming, "What took you so long?!!" Whatever the reason, I was happy they called and I still marvel at all of them calling the same afternoon and all of them calling two years after they had heard of me. The odds against that happening must be phenomenal. So, when you market, be patient. Your seeds may take a long time to sprout.

> Tip: You can also get mileage out of reprints of articles that someone else wrote about your prospects and clients. When you read the articles, cut them out and send them to the prospect or client with a brief note congratulating them. Better yet, call and congratulate them and, then, follow-up with the note and the copy of the article. That way you they get two exposures to you instead of just one.

The second decision you must make before you begin writing is where you will submit the article for publication. Which magazine? Which trade journal? Make sure that you are promoting yourself in places that will do you the most good. Becoming visible is important, but where you become visible is just as important. In fact, if you are visible in the wrong places, you are, essentially, invisible.

If you are targeting business owners, submit to the newspapers, magazines and journals they read. For example, if you are a consultant for accounting firms, you will get in your prospects' doors much more easily if you have written for the *Journal of Accountancy*, the publication of the American Institute of Certified Public Accountants.

To find out which journals they read, go back to the research you did on your target market. In addition, ask your prospects, current clients and their influencers what they read. There is no point in writing for a publication that your target market or their influencers don't read. Write for the publications they do read.

To find the contact names, addresses and phone numbers of magazines and trade journals, look in the following publications which are available at college libraries or in large public libraries.

Bacon's Newspaper/Magazine Directory (Two volumes)
Gale Directory of Publications and Broadcast Media

Matthews Media Directory
Standard Rate and Data Service (The volumes titled <u>Business Publications</u> and <u>Consumer Magazines</u>)
Working Press of the Nation (Four volumes)

In addition to going to the library, you can, for a fee, get this information on the Internet. Bacon's Newspaper/Magazine Directory and SRDS, Standard Rate and Data Service, each have Internet versions that can be accessed by the paid subscribers of their print editions.

If you already have a copy of a publication, you can find the contact information on the masthead. Once you have the names of the appropriate contact people, call or write the advertising and sales department and ask for a media kit.

Study the publications you are considering. What are their markets? Do their markets match your market. The media kit gives you demographic information. It provides a reader profile and circulation numbers. If your prospects or their influencers belong to a trade organization, contact it and request a new member kit. This will give you demographic information on the trade organization's members.

Influencers (doctors, lawyers, accountants, funeral directors, executives of retirement homes, etc.) all belong to trade organizations. Your target market may not read the trade journals published by these organizations, but the people they respect, admire and listen to read them. You want to be recommended by these influencers. You need to increase your visibility, build your credibility and create your desirability with them as well as with your target market.

Media kits and trade organization new member kits normally include an issue of the magazine or journal. If you find that the publication's readers are either your target market or the influencers of your target market, study the sample issue. Then, track down back issues to see the kind of subjects the publication covers. If your potential article doesn't cover one of these subjects, could you rework it so that it would? What topics have they covered in the past two years? Is there a topic they haven't covered or haven't covered recently that you could write about? If they have covered a topic recently, could you write about it from a different angle?

In addition to a sample of the publication, the media kit will usually include an editorial calendar which will tell you what topics are planned for future issues and when those issues will be released. This will help you plan the content and timing of an article submission. Media kits will tell you whether a publication is the right publication for you to include in your marketing efforts and it will help you figure out how and when to approach the publication with your proposed article.

The third decision you will make before you start to write is what the subject of your article will be. What can you write about as an expert? In Part Two, as you selected your target market, you studied your market's hopes and fears so that you could become the expert on them. What do they want to know? What do they need to know? What is being written on these topics now? What has been written recently? You want to write about a subject that is of great interest to your market, but you don't want to do something that has been done many times already. There's no point in being a me-too.

The fourth decision is the angle from which you will write the article. Look through back issues of the publication in order to see what topics have been covered in the past two years. What angle did each article take? If they have written extensively on your topic, can you approach it in a fresh way?

If you are a financial consultant, perhaps you are writing an article about the subject of financial planning. What angle do you take? Do you write about how to select a financial planner? How to save for retirement? How to save for your children's education? The relative weighting of stocks, bonds and mutual funds in a balanced portfolio? Value vs. growth in a stock portfolio? Which of these angles will best grab the attention of your target market?

When you went through the process of selecting your target market, you made a list of the benefits your market would get from doing business with you. Look back at your list. The benefits you listed are the same benefits your target market will receive from reading your article. This is the hook you will use to capture the editor's interest. To bait the hook, look at your title. Can you make it more eye-catching? To find ways of making it more eye-catching, go to a bookstore. What magazines catch your eye? Why? Study the covers. What headlines/article titles grab you? Write down all of the headlines that grabbed you. Why did each one catch your attention?

Now, look at the working title of your article. Is it a grabber? If not, change it. Your title has to grab the reader's attention so that he will want to read the article. As I wrote Top Dog, my working title was, Marketing Yourself for Sales Success.

Along the way, <u>Top Dog</u> was born. <u>Marketing Yourself for Sales Success </u>became the subtitle.

When you have a grab-them-by-the-throat, pop-their-eyeballs title and a statement of why your article would interest the editor's readers, you are ready to submit a query to him. You will find the editor's name on the masthead of the publication. Write him a letter. Do not call or fax. Tell him that your clients or their influencers read his magazine/journal. Tell him you have an idea for an article about a problem that his readers have. Ask if he would be interested in an article that offers a solution to that problem. If he says he is interested, he will probably ask you to send an outline of the article and clips of other articles you have had published. If he won't consider your article because you have never been published, write articles for local magazines or your local newspaper. Then, contact him again. If he is interested, send him an outline of your proposed article along with copies of the articles you have had published.

The fifth decision you must make is what the format of the article will be. What is the length of an article in a given publication? To find the answer to this question and all the other relevant information you need about the format the publication expects, write or call and ask for their publication guidelines. The guidelines will tell you the number of words an article should contain.

The sixth decision you will make is the timing of your article submission. Certain topics are time-sensitive. An article on how to find hidden tax deductions would have reader interest in January, not in August. An article on how to prevent the most common ski injuries won't have many readers in May. If your topic is time-sensitive, remember that there is generally a lead time of six to eight months between the time an editor selects an article and the time the article is published. This lead time has to be factored into your timing decision. Your tax article may interest the publisher in the Summer when he is looking ahead to his January issue. Similarly, your article on ski injuries may interest the editor in April for November publication. Many topics, however, are not time-sensitive. How to make money, how to reduce pain and how to improve your life are topics that are always in demand and are published all year.

WRITING AN ARTICLE

Once you have made the decisions on placement, subject, angle, format, timing and usage, you are ready to actually write the article and submit it for publication. You are probably saying to yourself, "If I could write, I'd be a writer, not a _____(fill in the blank.)" Don't worry. It's easier than you think. Just follow the old formula you learned in high school. Tell'em what you are going to tell'em (the introduction), tell'em (the body), tell'em what you told'em (the conclusion).

Writing is even easier than the formula suggests because the introduction and conclusion are usually no more than two or three sentences. In addition, the conclusion is really nothing more than a restating of your introduction.

That leaves the body of the article. At this point you may feel that you might as well be asked to write *War and Peace*, but writing the body of the article is not as difficult as it may at first appear. There are two reasons for this. First, your target market knows a lot less about the topic than you do. All you have to do is tell them what they need to know, not everything you know. Second, the human mind works best when asked to learn no more than three new pieces of information at a time. Therefore, the body of the article should contain no more than three ideas. This is what I call The Law of 3's.

The template for your article would look like this:

Introduction (Two or three sentences)

Body

  Key Idea #1
  Key Idea #2
  Key Idea #3

Conclusion (Two or three sentences that are the introduction in disguise.)

I'm sure you are beginning to realize you don't have the problem you thought you had. You thought your problem was, "How can I write enough information to fill an article?" Now you realize your problem is "How can I limit myself to just three ideas?" Instead of worrying about finding enough to say you have to worry about how to say less. A better problem, isn't it?

Select a topic for an article you could write. Ask yourself, "If I could tell my target market only one thing, what would I tell them?" This is Key Idea #1.

If you could tell them something else, what is the second thing you would tell your target market? That is Key Idea #2.

If you could tell them one more thing, what would you tell them? That is Key Idea #3.

Now go back. Look at your list. Are these really the three most important things you should tell them? Will they get what they desire or avoid what they fear if they use these three ideas? If not, choose three other ideas.

If you analyze what I have just written about how to write an article, what were the three key ideas I shared with you? If you listed them, they would be:

1) When you write an article, the format should be, "Tell'em what you are going to tell'em," "Tell'em," "Tell'em what you told'em."
2) The body of the article should contain no more than three key ideas which are the three things that your reader most needs to know.
3) Your two-or-three-sentence conclusion is a rewording of your two-or-three-sentence introduction.

You can use this high school English class formula, which I call The 3T Formula, to write any article on any subject. It solves the problem of length, one of the pre-writing decisions that you had to make. The amount you can write about each key point depends on the word count you are allowed in the publication's guidelines. If the publication's guidelines specify an article of 500 words, you will be able to write approximately 170 words on each key point. If the guidelines specify 1,000 words, you can write approximately 330 words on each key point.

If I were writing an article titled, "How to Write an Article," I could bare bones it and say, "Tell'em what you are going to tell'em, tell'em, tell'em what you told'em" and nothing more. If I had more space, I could explain how to write an introduction that grabs the reader's attention or how to phrase the conclusion so that it restates the introduction without using the exact same wording.

As you follow The 3T Formula you will find that writing an article is a lot easier than it looks. The preparation work takes longer than the actual writing.

Exercise:
Select one publication your target market reads.
Write for submission guidelines.
Study back issues of the publication.

Select a subject for an article that you want to submit to the publication.
Select the angle the article will take.
Answer these questions:

> What is the subject of my article?
> Why have I chosen it?
> What is the angle I have chosen?
> Why have I chosen it?
> What is the title of my article?
> Can I make it more eyeball-popping?
> What is my introduction?
> What is key point #1?
> What is key point #2?
> What is key point #3?
> What is my conclusion?

GETTING PUBLISHED

Once you have answered these questions about the article that you are writing, you have the ammunition you need to accomplish the last step—getting published. Editors buy solutions to their readers' problems. They are in business only because their readers, your prospects, benefit from the information in their publications. Of course, the word "buy" is used in a figurative sense. You won't get paid cash money until you are The Expert. Until then, you get paid in visibility, credibility and desirability and the value of that over your lifetime is incalculable. So is the value of PR. When you are published, not only will your ideas be in print to build your credibility as the expert, but your name, business name and business address will appear after the article so that prospects can call you and qualify themselves.

After you know you have information the publication's readers want, write or call the editor and explain how the information you have would be of interest to his readers. Your job is to present your article in such a way that the editor wants you. You may be the answer to an editor's prayer. They need first-rate, excellent articles to fill the pages of their publication. They can't fill it by themselves so they need you.

When you are ready to submit the article to an editor, remember that no publication will publish a poorly-written, grammatically-incorrect article, at least not any publications that would build your credibility. So, and this should go without saying, have your manuscript read for both content and grammar. Spell checkers and grammar checkers are good, but go only so far. After that you need a real person.

After your manuscript is typed, have it edited for typos and judged on appearance. It should look professional. This may sound petty, but everything, EVERYTHING, reflects on you. If I get a resume that has grammatical errors or is typed on flimsy "scratch" paper or is wrinkled or has a stain on it, I toss it. If your manuscript has errors, typos or an unprofessional appearance, the editor will toss it.

> TIP: When you submit an article, be sure to state that you are giving "one-time rights." That means the article is your property. You can submit the article to other publications later. Word of warning: Do not submit the same article to competing publications at the same time.

Include a photograph of yourself and a brief bio. This provides you with an additional marketing advantage since the readers will know how to find you.

Once you have been published, think leverage. How else can you use the article to market yourself?

Submit it to other publications.
Include it in your newsletter.
Include it in someone else's newsletter.
Send reprints to your clients.
Send reprints to your prospects.
Send reprints to their influencers.
Send reprints to your friends and relatives (hidden influencers.)
Include it in seminar packets.
Include it in speech handouts.
Use it as a chapter in your book.
Use it as a chapter in someone else's book.
Put it in your press kit.

While you have been increasing your visibility, you have also been building credibility by giving your readers information they can use. By the time you call them you have, hopefully, created desirability. They may actually want to talk to you.

While an article written by you helps establish you as the expert, an article written about you is also valuable. If it is written about your business, it is liquid gold because it gives you invaluable PR. An article is valuable even if it is not written about you as a businessperson. Perhaps you are featured in an article about volunteers for a golf tournament that raises money for camps for disabled children. When they mention you, they will most likely mention what you do for a living. That's one more exposure to help you stay in your prospects' minds. Every exposure you get adds to the snowballing effect.

In addition to writing an article, you can get your words published in other ways. You can write a letter to the editor, disagreeing or agreeing with a previously-published letter on a topic in your area of expertise. Or you can write a letter that offers new information or a new perspective on the subject. If you market yourself well, a reporter may interview you and write a follow-up piece and quote you.

For even more exposure, write a short piece for the Op-Ed page. The advantage of writing for this page is that your article is followed by your name, the town where you live and a brief job description. This end-of-article bio is a perfect marketing tool. It is a wonderful vehicle because a newspaper is generally read immediately, rather than getting lost in a magazine rack or in a stack on the coffee table. Appearing on the Op-Ed page gives you credibility. In essence, the newspaper has enhanced the image of you that you are working so hard to create.

NEWSLETTERS AS A MARKETING TOOL

You can also "get ink" by writing for newsletters. You can publish your own newsletter for clients, prospects and influencers or you can be a guest columnist in a newsletter published by someone else who sells to your target market. If you are a lawyer, you could be a guest columnist in a newsletter produced by an accountant. If you are a nature photographer, you could write a column on photographing gardens for a newsletter written by a landscape designer. Writing for someone else's newsletter has the added benefit of your receiving their implicit stamp of approval. After all, they wouldn't put you in their newsletter if they didn't think you were outstanding at what you do.

Writing your own newsletter has marketing advantages. First, you can send your words directly to the people you want to read them. Second, you can give a marketing opportunity to your target market's influencers who need to market themselves, too. This increases the likelihood that they will refer you. In addition, if they send the newsletter to their target market, you get exposure to everyone in their market.

I know what you are thinking. "First, I'm supposed to write an article. Now I'm supposed to write a newsletter. Give me a break. A little marketing is okay. I want to be a success, but I won't have time to sell if I spend all my time writing newsletters."

I agree. So, let me show you a simple process for producing a first-rate, business-generating newsletter.

Before I do that, I have to dispel some Nasty Newsletter Notions, as in "I have a notion to write me a newsletter, but these nasties keep gettin' in the way." "Nasties" are self-defeating beliefs that just aren't true. Let's look at these nasties and see why they aren't true. A newsletter is too valuable a marketing tool to let a few nasties stop you from producing one.

Nasty #1: "Newsletters are small newspapers."

A newsletter is not a newspaper. It doesn't contain news. It shouldn't contain news because news would date it and severely shorten its usable life. Instead, it contains helpful information that is not time-sensitive. A newsletter is actually a big self-help column. The articles in it are written to help your readers solve their problems and improve their lives.

The only similarity to a newspaper is the existence of headlines. As in a newspaper, the headline has to grab the reader's attention and make him want to read the article. To see the difference between an effective and an ineffective headline compare these headlines. "Save 25% on your advertising costs" or "Reduce your expenses." "Save 25% on your advertising costs" grabs a reader's attention. If you pay for advertising, spending 25% less would be fantastic. In contrast, "Reduce your expenses" is a lot easier to slide right past. It doesn't shout the benefit the way the first headline does. Good headlines shout, "This will solve your problem!"

Nasty #2: "Newsletters are short books."

When you think of a newsletter, think "letter," not book." People are pressed for time and we are a culture accustomed to sound bytes. If your newsletter is long, it may end up on the "I'll read it later" pile. Usually that's the pile nearest the wastebasket. An eight-page newsletter is usually too long and the recipient puts off reading it, perhaps indefinitely. A four-page newsletter is usually just right. It stands a good chance of being read.

The articles themselves should be short, too. The three-key-idea format you use for articles becomes the one-key-idea rule for newsletters. The shorter the article, the greater the chance that it will be read. The recipients didn't buy the newsletter (in most cases.) They didn't ask for it. Even if they did, they are still pressed for time. Make your newsletter readable in short blocks. A newsletter with short articles and good use of white space invites reading.

Nasty #3: "Newsletters are sole creations."

A newsletter can be written solely by you, but doesn't have to be. It can contain guest columns, question and answer columns and previously-published graphics and articles that you have permission to reprint. You can even buy a newsletter that is produced by an independent company for your industry or one that is produced by your company and bears your name and title on the masthead. In fact, if you are an intrapreneur who works for a large company, you may not be allowed to send out any newsletter except the company-produced or company-sanctioned newsletter.

Nasty #4: "Newsletters are totally original."

A newsletter doesn't have to contain only completely new, never-before-seen material that no one else knows. There's no way it could. All you have to do is give the readers another exposure to information they already know, but may have forgotten or show them how to do what they are already doing in a faster or less expensive or more effective way. The material that you include in the newsletter simply has to solve problems that your clients and prospects have. The goal of the newsletter is to help establish your credentials as The Expert. You are seen as The Expert when you know what your readers need to know and you bring them that information.

Nasty #5: "Newsletters are regular."

A newsletter does not have to come out on a set schedule. A newsletter comes out whenever you want to put it out. Monthly is great. So is quarterly. Even occasionally is acceptable. A newsletter's success depends far more on how long you keep publishing it than on how many times a year you publish it. Two years is a minimum trial period for a newsletter. It will take that long to be able to start to measure its effectiveness. Even then, the point at which the business you gain from a newsletter begins to outweigh the expense of producing and mailing the newsletter can never be accurately measured. It is just one more piece of the marketing pie. It gives you one more exposure to your target market. It provides one more example of your credibility. It raises you one degree higher on the desirability scale. Rarely will you get a client as a direct result of the newsletter. A well-done newsletter, however, will always be one of the pieces that tips the scale in your favor.

Now that these Nasty Newsletter Notions have been proven to be false, you are ready to produce your newsletter. As you begin writing the Practically Perfect Newsletter, remember that the operative word is well-done. A newsletter is well-done if it is concise, contains compelling information, has a consistency in appearance and is a credit to you as The Expert.

PRODUCING A NEWSLETTER

If you follow these six steps, you will find that producing a newsletter can be a practically painless process. Please don't skip any of them. The more steps you skip, the more painful the process becomes.

Remember the time you carried that tall stack of boxes from the car to the house because you didn't want to make two trips? The stack wobbled. As you tried to steady the boxes, you tripped over the bicycle that had been left on the floor of the garage. As the boxes came tumbling down, you hit the concrete floor. The score was Floor 1, Knee 0. The shattered glasses inside the boxes looked like bone fragments inside your knee.

Shortcuts take more time in the end and often add additional expense. As with life, so with newsletters. You can't be Top Dog lying on the floor, embarrassed. So, please follow the process.

Step One: List one hundred topics that you could cover in your newsletter.

One hundred may seem like a lot, but you will need as many ideas for articles as you can get since the success of your newsletter will come because it appears repeatedly over a long period of time. For example, if you are a marketing consultant, you might list these topics:

1) mailing lists
2) seminars
3) marketing plans

Step Two: For each topic write a headline that will grab the reader.

1) Stop calling my dog!
2) The story of the empty chair
3) Plan to fail.

Step Three: Study as many newsletters as you can.

The subject matter isn't important. Talk to the people who publish newsletters that you think are good. Ask them to share their advice on what to do and what not to do. Learning from other people's mistakes is far less expensive than learning from your own. Also study bad newsletters. Studying bad newsletters is as helpful as studying good newsletters because bad newsletters show you what not to do.

Step Four: Analyze each good newsletter.

List the features that you like. Do you like the

1) writing style
2) length of articles
3) use of white space
4) font style
5) font size
6) use of humor
7) statistical information
8) lay-out
9) paper (color, size and texture)
10) ink color
11) newsletter name
12) article titles (headlines)
13) photographs
14) clip art
15) cartoons
16) charts
17) graphs

18) drawings
19) guest columnists
20) Q & A column?

After you have done this with each of the newsletters you will have a strong sense of how you want to structure your newsletter. By combining the elements you find most appealing, your newsletter will most likely be appealing to your readers, too.

Step Five: Make a list of people you would like to have write for your newsletter.

List as many people as you can. Keep in mind as you do this that you are entering a potential minefield. If they appear in your newsletter, ipso facto, you are endorsing them. If someone uses their services and is disappointed, it reflects poorly on you. So, write down as many potential contributors as you can, but be careful. When you ask them to write for your newsletter, protect yourself.

First, don't ask them to write a column. Ask them to write one article. If they write well, you can always ask them to become a regular contributor. If they don't, you are saved the embarrassment of having to "unask" them. Second, ask them if they would have any objections if you edited their column to fit the newsletter's style. Assure them that you won't change the substance of their words. Doing this allows you to fix grammatical errors and typos. In fact, for the sake of good relations, if asked you can refer to any grammatical error as a typo.

In addition to guest contributors, you can also get help from your readers. After all, you want them to want to read your newsletter. You can ask them to submit questions for your Q & A column. (Hint: If no one does initially, write the questions yourself and "submit" them.) Ask your readers to tell you what topics they would like you to cover. Ask them what their problems are. Ask them for any unique solutions they have found for problems that all your readers have.

Step Six: Make a list of printers along with their prices.

One way to compile a list of good printers is to look again at the newsletters you admire. Ask who printed each of them.

> Word of caution: If the quality of the print job isn't first rate, the price is too expensive. The price is too expensive even if it is the cheapest price in town.

This takes us back to the concept of the well-done newsletter. Your newsletter is you. Period. It represents your thinking and level of expertise. It also represents the quality of your work. Some people won't mind if there are typos or grammatical errors or if their names are spelled incorrectly on the address label or if the newsletter is stapled crookedly.

Some people won't mind. Other people are like me. If your newsletter isn't absolutely first-rate, I assume, probably correctly, that your work isn't either. I won't hire you. I won't recommend you. After the first disappointment, I probably won't even read you. Do you want to do a mediocre job and hope that your best clients and prospects and their influencers are among "some" people or do you want to do a first-rate job and know that the odds are good that your best clients and prospects and their influencers are among all those "other" people, the ones who loathe shoddy work?

Once you have completed these six steps, you will have:

Chosen article topics for your newsletter.
Written attention-grabbing headlines for the articles.
Found the best way to produce a newsletter and the mistakes to avoid.
Selected an eye-catching format.
Reduced your workload by finding guest columnists.
Selected a printer.

You are ready to produce a first-rate newsletter. It doesn't seem as overwhelming as it did, does it?

Tip: Don't date your newsletter. Instead put Roman numerals on each issue. If your newsletter is undated, you can get mileage out of it for a long time. Also, don't include dated material like seminar announcements. Instead, put these in a separate insert. Not only will it keep the newsletter from becoming dated, but it will also increase the chances that the seminar will be attended. The insert can be pulled out and posted as a reminder of the seminar, rather than read and forgotten.

Now there is just one thing left to do. Distribute your newsletter. You are looking for people who will read it and quote from it and pass it on. To make sure this happens do not buy a mailing list. Repeat. Do Not Buy a Mailing List. My dog may be on it. My dog gets mail. My dog gets phone calls. My dog gets invitations. She received an invitation to a one-day, $350 seminar. Unfortunately, she already had plans for the day. Otherwise, I was sorely tempted to drive her there and help her sign-in. Do you want to invite my dog to your seminar? Do you want to waste time calling my dog? Do you want to send my dog your newsletter?

Don't buy lists. If you buy a list, her name may be on it. Even if you're lucky and it isn't, every third person in town who does what you do has purchased the same list. Make your own list. Your list can include your clients, prospects who have called for information or sent in a reply card seeking information, prospects who have attended a seminar and prospects who registered for a seminar but did not attend. Always seek new prospects to add to your list. Ask people to take an action that shows that they are prospects. For example, if you are a photographer, you could offer a free tip sheet on photographing babies to people who send in a stamped, self-addressed envelope. When they do, you have a list of prospects who are interested in what you do. Similarly, if you offer a free class in scrapbooking, names of the attendees can be added to your list. Be a detective who is always looking for ways to add prospect names to your own homemade list.

Another way to find names for your list is to speak to organizations. When you speak to an organization, it is permissible to ask for a list of their members. This membership list now becomes part of your newsletter list. This list is free and can be used as many times as you like. When you buy a list from a broker, you are buying one-time use. To make sure that you don't use the list more than once, the list is salted with the names of the broker's mother and his brother's cat. That way they know if you have used the list illegally after the one authorized use.

ALTERNATIVE INK

Once you can produce articles and a newsletter, it truly is not far from there to writing a book. Enough articles printed in magazines, enough articles printed in newsletters, enough articles printed in trade journals and you have sufficient material for a book, possibly more than one. If your newsletter is designed with a recurrent column, for example a column on customer service training, you have a collection of columns that can easily be turned into a book.

To reach your market you can write a book that is designed specifically for this market as my book is designed specifically for professional service providers. Target your book narrowly so that your market knows that you are talking to it. Talk about issues that concern your market and problems that they have. Of course, before you write a book look at what is already out there. If what you would say has already been said, consider writing a book about other topics that are of interest to your market.

There is not enough space in this book to discuss the process of writing a book. That is a whole book in itself. I would be remiss, however, not to raise a major point about publishing the book you write. The question every author must answer is, "Should I try to find a publisher for my book or should I self-publish?"

The answer is, "It depends." If you self-publish, the costs are all yours, but so are the profits. If you self-publish, you will do all the marketing for your book. If you self-publish, you have total control over the end product. If someone else publishes, they have nearly total control over the end product. They have most of the profit, but, then, they have all of the costs. They will do some of the marketing, but you will still have to do most of it unless you are already a best-selling author. To make the decision somewhat easier, POD, print on demand, is gaining in popularity and respect. You self-publish, but do not have to upfront the cost. You pay for the design and layout. The print "run" consists of only one to five books. After that you can order as many books as you want at discounted prices. You do not have to pay for a minimum run of one thousand books as a self-published author used to have to do. POD means that an author will no longer face the possibility of having a garage full of unsold books. I personally know two authors who do.

In deciding whether or not to self-publish, ask yourself:

Can I afford to pay to have the book edited, designed and printed?

Do I want to have ultimate responsibility for editing the book, designing the cover, laying out the book, proofing the book, printing the book and marketing the book?

Do I have the time, desire, ability and money to do all the marketing of my book?

How adamant am I about having total control over the end product?

Am I better at working to deadline if it is externally-imposed (ie., the publisher's deadline) vs. internally-imposed (ie., my deadline)?

Your answers to these questions will guide your thinking as you face this publishing dilemma. To help you make your decision you might want to read these excellent books:

The Self-Publishing Manual: How to Write, Print & Sell Your Own Book by Dan Poynter

The Complete Guide to Self-Publishing: Everything You Need to Know to Write, Publish, Promote and Sell Your Own Book by Tom and Marilyn Ross

THE POWER OF THE TESTIMONIAL LETTER

The pen is one of the most powerful tools you have in your ongoing campaign to create the perception of you as The Expert. The pen is powerful even when you don't wield it. In fact, it is more powerful then.

One of the most powerful things that can add to the perception of you as the expert is a testimonial letter. It removes one of the biggest, if not the biggest reason, that people won't do business with you. That reason is fear. If other people have used your services and were so pleased that they sing your praises, the prospect feels less fearful.

What would you do if you were looking for a new dentist or doctor or insurance agent? Most of us would ask our friends. If one or more of our friends raved about someone, we would probably give that person a try.

Along with verbal testimonials you need written testimonials for your business. Put them in a notebook that potential clients can read. As they do, they may see the names of people they know. When I was considering booking a hotel for an event, the banquet manager handed me his testimonial book. I recognized two names among the letters. One was a person connected with the Chamber of Commerce. I reasoned that, if the Chamber was delighted with a function they held at the hotel, I probably would be, too.

Testimonials answer objections before they are raised. People who don't know you are afraid to do business with you no matter how personable you are or how professional your sales literature is. They may not be happy with where they are right now. Their tooth may ache. Their retirement funds may be insufficient. Their back may hurt. They may not be happy, but they are afraid you might make the situation worse.

Since testimonial letters are literally worth their weight in gold, why doesn't every professional use testimonials? They don't use them primarily because they don't want to ask for them. They feel awkward. They feel they would be imposing on the client. Actually, your best clients would love to be asked, especially if you offer to write the letter for them so all they have to do is put it on their stationery. I did this for one of my clients. She then went on and made the letter even better. The collaborative effort produced a whiz-bang letter. Your clients may be intimidated by coming up with a letter from scratch, but they are usually more than willing to either copy your letter or use it as the base for their own letter.

When you write a testimonial letter for a client, remember that the letter should not rave about you. It should rave about what you did for the client. If you tell people you are a fantastic estate lawyer, it is bad marketing. If your clients tell them you are a fantastic estate lawyer, it is good marketing. If your clients tell them you are a fantastic estate lawyer because you reduced their future estate tax by 43%, it is incredible marketing.

If the client wants to write the letter himself but is not sure what to include, give him a couple of samples of testimonial letters. Then, ask him questions to get him thinking about the benefits he gained from working with you. If you are a marketing consultant, ask him if his marketing costs went down after working with you for three months. If he says, "Yes," ask him to tell how much in the letter. Ask him if his sales went up. If he says, "Yes," ask him to tell how much. For example, if his sales increased 34% last quarter after he followed your marketing recommendations, ask him to put that in his letter. If you are a chiropractor and reduced the pain in someone's hip, ask him how the reduction in pain has affected his life. If he says he missed only two days of work last month because of the pain in his hip rather than the eleven days he missed the month before, ask him to put that in his letter. When they write their testimonial letters, you want your clients to focus on the results they got from working with you. Using numbers and percentages gives the results greater impact and makes them more believable. The more specific the benefit the more believable it is.

If you haven't asked for testimonials before, start asking today. Call at least one client a week. Start with the clients that you feel most comfortable with. Once you have had success with them you will begin to feel comfortable with the process. Asking for testimonials should become part of your ongoing marketing plan.

Quotes from your testimonial letters can be used again (leverage) in brochures and sales letters. Similarly, you can use comments from evaluations you asked for after you did seminars. Names cannot be used with these since you don't have permission, but the statement can be quoted and attributed to an identifiable group.

For example, the quote might be from the VP of Marketing at a Fortune 500 company. You can't give his name or the name of the company, but you can identify the quote as having been made by "the VP of Marketing of a Fortune 500 company." Unless the prospect either knows him personally or he is famous, his name doesn't matter, anyway, but his position does.

THE POWER OF THE SPOKEN WORD

There is another marketing tool that is as powerful as the pen. The power of the pen is equaled by the power of the voice. Just as there are no unseen, invisible experts, there are no unheard, silent experts. Two of the best ways to use your voice to build credibility are to make speeches and to conduct seminars. If you are a person who doesn't like to speak, you can still use the power of the voice. When you finish this chapter, you still may not want to speak, but you will be confident of your ability to do so.

Top Dog is always confident. That confidence comes not from how great he is, but from how great he makes his clients feel and from the great job he does for them. The spotlight is not on him. It is on what he can do and does do for his target market. He puts the focus on them. He is not the stereotypical nervous speaker gripping the podium with shaking hands. He is confident and relaxed.

In addition to being confident, he is knowledgeable. He knows his target market inside and out. He knows the best marketing tools to use to reach the market. If speaking is one of his marketing tools, he knows the best way to create and deliver a successful speech. If you follow his strategy for making a speech, you will, too.

STRATEGY FOR A SUCCESSFUL SPEECH

1. Know the audience.

Speaking to the audience's needs/fears/pain is a key factor in a speech's success. A speech that does not address the audience's needs is not a successful speech no matter how technically perfect it is.

You have already done research on your target market. You know who they are. You know what they desire and what they fear. You know what the "hot" topics are in the publications they read. These topics are "hot" because the readers want to know about them.

You can supplement your knowledge simply by asking for more information. If you are part of the program of an organization, ask the program director for an audience profile. When you mingle with the audience before your speech, ask them what they want to learn from you. Mingling is fun and meeting them before the speech will make you more comfortable when you are speaking.

2. Use the Law of 3's.

In our desire to help the audience we often create information overload. Instead, use the Law of 3's. Present no more than three ideas or one idea with three supporting points. Our minds cannot absorb more than three ideas at one time. If you try to include more information than they can absorb, your listeners will become confused or bored during your talk and tune out.

In our desire to help the audience we often try to tell them everything they need to know. They can't absorb all that information. It is like trying to pour a gallon of water down the throat of a man who is dying of thirst. Sure he needs the gallon—eventually. Now he can handle only an ounce.

3. Use visuals.

I should add the words "with care." Visuals can be props as well as charts and slides. I vividly remember a presentation on time management. The speaker was holding an unusually large metal tape measure as he spoke. To emphasize a point he asked a volunteer from the audience to grab the end of the tape measure, walk across the stage with it and let go of the end. Because the tape was taut it remained sticking straight out across the width of the stage after the volunteer let go of the end. Then, the speaker cut the tape measure using a pair of scissors. A piece of the metal tape flew across the stage. This was a big mistake. First, the flying metal posed a danger to the "helper" and the audience members sitting close to the stage. Second, it didn't reinforce the point he was trying to make. The flying metal made such an impression that I remember it, but I don't remember the point that it was intended to reinforce. While a good action visual is usually more powerful than a slide, it has drawbacks. If all you remember is the visual and don't remember the point that it was meant to illustrate, the visual didn't do its job.

Many presenters use slides. It is the visual aid most often used and most often misused. If you use slides, make sure they are necessary. Ask yourself, "Will the audience understand my point without this slide?" If the answer is "Yes," don't use it.

When you do use slides, ask yourself these questions. Why am I using a slide here? Is this slide necessary to make my point? Would a three-dimensional visual work better? If you are going to use a slide with text as opposed to a slide with a photograph or drawing, ask yourself if the text on the slide would be visible from the back of the room. We have all sat through presentations where the only people who could read the slides were the people in the front of the room.

4. Grab their attention.

Humor can be a powerful tool, if used well. It can open doors for you. However, the chance that the humor you select will hurt you is far greater than the chance that it will help you. A joke might not be appropriate for the subject matter or it might inadvertently offend someone. Instead of beginning with a joke, open with a story or a statistic that is surprising or a short quiz. Then tell'em what you are gong to tell them so they will want to listen. Use your first words to open a door into the audience's minds. Don't take the chance of using humor that could backfire and slam the door in your face. First impressions are powerful and extremely difficult to change.

5. Tell stories.

The best speakers are storytellers. Stories speak to us in ways that factual information never can. Tell a story about a client you helped. Talk about the problem that client had and how, specifically, you helped him solve the problem. If your listener has the same problem, he recognizes himself in the story. Keep your stories short. They are told to illustrate a point and should be easy-to-follow and easy-to-remember. Often stories are the only things the audience will remember so they should very clearly make your point.

6. Practice, practice, practice.

And then practice some more. When you practice, practice how you want to say it, but don't practice the exact wording. Practice until it is perfect. Doing it wrong sixteen times won't make it right. Whenever I hear the words "doing it wrong," I remember Michael Keaton delivering his children to school in the movie, "Mr. Mom." He is scolded by the safety guard who tells him, "You're doing it wrong." The audience laughs. We can all identify with him. We have all "done it wrong." When you practice your speech, "do it right." What you do in practice is what you will do in performance.

To see if you are "doing it right" watch yourself in the mirror when you are practicing. Then, ask someone to videotape you. Watch the tape many times. Each time you will pick up on something else that you did wrong or could do better. Make an audio tape, too. Close your eyes and you can hear whether or not you had enough vocal variety. The video and audio tapes are amazing resources in helping you "do it right."

By watching the video or even just watching yourself in a mirror, you can critique yourself by asking the following questions.

> Did I change pace—slow/fast?
> Did I change pitch—high/low?
> Did I change volume—soft/loud?
> Did I pause? Most speakers don't pause often enough or long
> enough.
> Did I hold my head straight or tilted to the side?
> Did I use my hands or keep them in my pockets or stuck to the front of my
> clothing in the fig leaf position?
> Did I fidget, play with my hands, play with my hair, rustle my notes?
> Did I use appropriate gestures?
> Were they big enough to be seen?
> Did I ruin my speech with "ahs," "ums," "wells" and "you
> knows?"

> Tip: Pausing adds emphasis, grabs the reader's attention and prevents us from delivering at machine gun pace. We always speak more quickly when we deliver the speech than we did in practice. A pause breaks our headlong gallop through the material.

Don't practice the speech word for word. Instead practice making your points. Trying to remember exact wording guarantees problems like fear of forgetting, loss of concentration and loss of eye contact as you look up or down or to the side to access information. If you forget a word in a memorized speech, you may freeze and find yourself unable to continue.

Your goal is to deliver a speech that is audience-appropriate and first-rate. Practicing will allow you to dispense with notes, relax and be "spontaneous." The more you practice the more "spontaneous" you will appear.

7. Watch the clock.

Use no more than the time that has been allotted to you. Always finish at the appointed hour or, preferably, before. Do you remember how thrilled you were when a teacher let you out of class early? We are still children inside. We like to be let out early.

In order to be able to do this, you might want to use a technique I developed to use in my speeches. Write the speech with one part that can be omitted if you are running overtime. You can write your speech so that it sounds perfectly fine with or without that section.

8. Be adaptable.

When you work the room before your speech, ask the people what they hope to learn that evening. If their answers are similar and they are not what you planned on covering, change your speech. You know your topic well enough to change the angle and still get your message across.

A prepared speech can be changed at the last minute if it isn't memorized. If it is memorized, any change will throw you completely off-track. Find a place in the speech where you can remove some material and put in the material the audience wants covered. If you know your key points, your statistics, your stories and your exercises, you can weave them into a new cloth.

You may also want to change your speech in response to the actions of the audience. Watch your audience. Listen to them. Observe their body language. Always be prepared to change. Are they restless? Are they talking to each other? Do they look bored? Are they looking at their watches? Do they look confused? Any of these situations require changes in your presentation. You may decide to cut out sections in order to end earlier. You might decide to inject some humor or add an interactive exercise. A good speech is a dynamic, not static, situation. It may need to be changed right before it is given or even while it is being given.

9. Enjoy yourself.

If you are enjoying the speech yourself, the audience will, too. To make the speech an enjoyable, rather than a stressful, situation you can employ these calming techniques.

Work the room. Before your presentation try to talk to as many people as possible so that you are not speaking to a room filled with strangers.

Focus on the audience. Put the focus on how you can help the audience and not on how nervous you are.

Tell stories. Human beings were weaned on stories from the days of the earliest cavemen. We love stories.

Be yourself. Trying to be someone else will always make you feel uncomfortable. If you are naturally humorous, be humorous. If you are bubbly, be bubbly. If you are measured and logical, be measured and logical. Trying to assume someone else's persona is a guarantee of failure. Your awkwardness will show. If the audience recognizes the persona, their regard for you will slip. I listened to a keynote speaker at a corporate meeting. He did everything "right." The only problem is that he was a clone of an extremely well-known national speaker. I felt like I was watching a parody of the national speaker. The speaker's words were lost on me because I became focused on the quality of his " impersonation," not on his message. I spent the entire speech noticing all the mannerisms and movements and ideas he had "borrowed." I wondered what he would have been like if he had been himself.

10. Make eye contact.

Slowly move your eyes around the room making eye contact with everyone. Be sure to do this slowly, lingering on each person for a least a few seconds. Try to look directly at each person more than once during the speech. If you find it difficult to look directly at someone, look at a spot on their forehead just above the bridge of their nose. They'll never know that that is where you are looking. They will think that you are looking directly at them

11. Be enthusiastic.

Your enthusiasm keeps the audience interested. Enthusiasm is an amazing thing. It not only keeps the audience interested, but a speaker's enthusiasm actually creates enthusiasm in the audience. Enthusiasm is contagious. If you are excited and think your idea is the greatest thing since sliced bread, they may, too.

If you want to have enthusiasm when you speak, you will need to practice with enthusiasm. We are never any better during the presentation than we were during practice. If you practice your speech without feeling, that's how you will deliver it.

12. Be animated.

Move. Smile. Laugh. Think of the boring presenters you have watched. Did they move? Were they animated? Did they smile? Laugh? Cry? Chuckle? Did they even appear to be breathing?!

The most boring presenter I ever listened to was a man who projected slides chock-full of text unto a wall. At the beginning of the presentation he walked up to the wall and read us every word on every slide. At the end of the "presentation" he turned around. He showed as much animation facing us as he did with his back turned to us. Sadly, I am not making this up. The presentation was so boring that the only thing I learned was that I shouldn't sit in the front row where an inconspicuous exit is not possible.

This is an extreme example, but we have all seen presenters like him. Deadwood does not captivate an audience. As one of the members of the audience said after the presentation, "That was right up there with watching paint dry." Personally, I would have preferred watching the paint. Be animated. Move when you speak, but move slowly. People don't want to stare at deadwood, but neither do they want to keep swiveling their heads from side to side as though they were trying to follow the ball in a tennis match. Be animated enough to hold your audience's attention, but not so animated that your movements are a distraction rather than an attraction.

13. Call for action.

Ask your audience to act. Ask them to write things down. What we do we remember. I remember a luncheon meeting of a group of sales professionals. We were asked to extract objects from our purses and pockets. We became part of the presentation rather than just sitting and listening passively.

You need to involve the audience in order to reach them. Every audience is composed of three types of people: auditories, visuals and kinesthetics. Auditories process information best if they can hear it. Visuals process information best if they can see it or read it. Kinesthetics process information best if they can touch it. Hence, they need to write down information.

We are not purely one type or the other. I am a visual with a strong kinesthetic secondary. In order to learn something I have to read it and then write the information down. I can't learn if I don't do both. Hearing is a poor way for me to learn. I can't process the information so I don't learn it. I am the proverbial "in one ear and out the other" learner.

14. Sell solutions.

I attended a dinner meeting of Women in Finance, a local group composed of women in the financial services industry. (Go where your target market is!) The speaker, a university professor, was scheduled to speak for 45 minutes. He rambled in a disjointed fashion for seventeen minutes and ended with these words, "Tom and Mary from _____ Bookstore are at the table over there. Go buy one of my books."

I wish I could say that I am exaggerating when I tell this story, but I'm not. The speaker used the speech as an occasion for blatant, crass commercialism. I didn't buy a book and I didn't buy him, either. He wasn't interested in the audience or their problems. Not surprisingly, his short speech was ill-prepared, rambling and boring. We came to hear a first-rate, well-prepared, enthusiastically-delivered speech. We didn't come to be bored or exploited. Sell a solution to the audience's problems, not your books.

15. Work with what you've got.

If you rent a room for a seminar, you can control the set-up of the room: lectern/no lectern, mike/no mike, handheld mike/hands-free mike, chair and table set-up, position of sign-in table, position of projection screen, size of room, location of room. If a group has invited you to speak, you have little control. They may ask you for your preferences. These preferences may or may not be what you get.

Often you will be speaking in far from ideal conditions. I remember speaking once in a very long, narrow room with windows along one end. I had to speak from the other end of the room. Everyone, except the people at the two front tables, had difficulty seeing me because of a series of poles that ran down the center of the room. The people who were seated at the other end of the room literally needed binoculars to see me.

What do you do when you find yourself in a similar situation? Punt. Graciously. Make the best of what you have and smile!

16. Leave them needing you.

If you tell your audience everything you know, they will leave believing that they know everything they need to know. They won't think they need you. Leave them wanting more. Leave them with questions. Leave them eager to talk with you, one-on-one. Leave them feeling that they need to talk with you.

17. Ask for feedback.

Always ask the members of the audience to fill out an evaluation form. Since you want them to fill out the forms and return them, give them an incentive to do it right then. I announce a drawing for a door prize and tell them that my assistant will pick up the forms, put them in a hat and I will draw one for the prize. At this point I hold up a wrapped "gift" so that their curiosity is piqued.

Keep the evaluation form short. Five questions are a good number. Most evaluation forms use number scales. These don't give the best information because an 8 out of 10 means "very good" to one person and just "good" to another. Even an evaluation form that uses "Excellent," "Good," "Fair," and "Poor" doesn't give you information about what the listener liked or didn't like and why.

Instead ask questions that elicit information. Good questions are:

> What did you find most helpful about the presentation?
> What changes could I make to improve the presentation?
> What questions do you have that the presentation didn't cover?
> What topic would you like to see covered in a future presentation?
> Would you like to receive a free report on _____?

This last question serves two purposes. First, it shows you the level of interest in a specific topic. If they aren't interested, they won't want the free report. Second, it flags the respondent as a qualified prospect.

SEMINARS AS A MARKETING TOOL

Seminars are one of the most effective marketing tools for a professional service provider. In fact, it is the perfect showcase for your talents. Seminars attract people who are predisposed to buy what you sell; otherwise, they wouldn't come to the seminar. You get to talk to a room full of qualified prospects. That's the marketing equivalent of Paradise!

Your purpose for the seminar should be to create qualified prospects, not to sell. To accomplish this the seminar should educate, not pitch products. Education is a door-opener. It is an extremely effective marketing tool. As with writing articles, you don't have to re-invent the wheel. The information you are giving is information that your competitors could give. That doesn't matter. What matters is that you are the one giving it.

Your market wants to be educated. That's why seminars can be an excellent marketing tool. I say "can be" because they can also be a waste of time and money and energy. It all depends on whether or not you do them correctly. A bad seminar will unmarket you along with wasting your time, money and effort. The motto of the successful seminar producer is, "Do it right or don't do it at all."

After you are comfortable speaking in public, a seminar is easy. It is simply talking longer. A seminar gives you visibility, credibility and desirability in one package. If you are not a polished presenter, it is still possible to do an outstanding seminar. You can bring in an out-of-town expert. You welcome the participants.

You introduce the out-of-town expert. (the oot, for short) You close the program after the oot speaks. You are the expert on your market and their needs. After all, you brought in the oot.

Better yet, try being the oot yourself. It isn't as hard as it looks. Remember how you structured the article you wrote using the 3 T Formula? You used the 3 T Formula and The Law of Threes. The 3 T Formula (Tell'em what you are going to tell'em. Tell'em. Tell'em what you told them.) provided the format for your article. The Law of Threes (three key ideas in the body of the article) provided the content. You wrote your article using the two laws and you wrote your speech using them. Now you can use them to write your seminar. The difference between a speech and a seminar is nothing more than a difference in length and the difference between a monologue and a dialogue.

You talk longer so, as with longer articles, you put in more words. You say more about each of the three points. Since it is a dialogue, you build in audience participation in the form of short exercises that the participants do. You want them to leave excited about the process and knowing that they need you.

A tremendous amount of money is wasted on seminars that do not achieve their goal. They do not result in prospects that call and ask to do business with you. To make sure you don't waste your money, this section includes detailed instructions and extensive checklists. If you follow them exactly, your seminar will yield highly-qualified prospects. If you don't, you will pay a lot of money to fill a room with empty chairs and buy expensive refreshments for the people you had hoped would be sitting in those chairs.

A seminar that is poorly-attended will yield few future sales. That makes the cost of each sale very high. If you get no sales, of course, the seminar is an absolute waste of time and money. If you don't get people to the seminar or you don't have a means to follow-up after the seminar or you have the means to follow-up, but don't do it, you turn one of the world's best PR tools into a costly flop.

The first decision you need to make is also one of the most important decisions. You need to select a seminar topic. In selecting your topic focus on your market's most pressing problems. The more pain they have, the more they want the relief your seminar can offer.

When you select a seminar topic, don't be a me-too. If you open your morning newspaper and out fall four sheets of yellow paper each announcing a seminar on "saving for your child's college education," why in the world would you pay for an identical sheet of colored paper to announce a seminar you are sponsoring on "saving for your child's college education?"

Either choose a different topic, "Ten Ways to Disguise Dog Food—Cooking in Your Retirement Years" or a different angle, "Preparing Your Child for a Career in Fast Food." Of course, most of you wouldn't try headlines that are that audacious, but it sure beats being a yellow paper newspaper insert me-too. Remember, first you have to grab the prospects' eyeballs and make-em pop. Then, you may have a chance for the serious stuff. Your topic may be the most wonderful topic in the world, but, unless the title of the seminar entices them to come, they'll never know it.

In designing your presentation, educate; don't make a sales pitch. The audience came to learn. Of course, you hope that the education they receive from you will create a desire to buy. The whole purpose of the seminar is to identify highly-qualified prospects that want to meet with you after the seminar. Care must be taken, though, to give the prospects what they came for—solutions to their problems.

To increase the likelihood that they will call you after the seminar involve them. Make their seminar experience active, not passive. Build an interactive presentation. The more interactive the presentation, the more your audience will like it and you. The activities should appeal to each of the learning styles, visual, auditory and kinesthetic. Use props, like slides and flip charts, to reach the visuals, stories to reach the auditories and hands-on participation, like making a list, filling in blanks or taking an action, to reach the kinesthetics.

No matter how good your presentation is, it should end before the audience's attention span does. Keep the time to no longer than one hour—30 minutes for presentation and 30 minutes for questions. Always leave them wanting more. That's what will induce them to meet with you.

You need to have a way for highly-qualified prospects in the audience to identify themselves. For example, tell you them that you have an information booklet available. If they are interested, all they have to do is write "booklet" on the back of their business card or write their name and address and the word "booklet" on an index card that you have provided and bring it up to you after the seminar. That way you get face to face with highly-qualified prospects. They qualified themselves first by coming to the seminar and second by requesting your booklet.

That's marketing gold. Their names should immediately be added to your prospect list. Remember, you make your own list. You never buy a list. As a bonus, you get to talk with these highly-qualified prospects face-to-face when they come up to give you the card. Needless to say, mail the requested booklet to them the next day.

Be in control. Ask the audience to submit questions on index cards. Have an assistant bring up the cards at the end of the seminar. Before the seminar write some questions on cards that your assistant can add to the audience's cards. That way you will be sure to be asked the questions you want to answer. If you take questions directly from the audience, rather than from cards, repeat the question before you answer it so that everyone in the audience hears the question. If there are questions you want to answer that the audience didn't ask, you can introduce your own questions by saying, "Let me share a couple of other questions that audiences have asked me."

Always be the last person to speak. After the question and answer session, close with one interesting piece of information that they didn't get in the seminar. This guarantees that their last impression is of you as the expert.

End the seminar with a call to action: write—call—come in—send for. In fact, every marketing activity you do should end with a call to action. For example, if you send a newsletter, ask them to e-mail you or call you to obtain a free report that you are offering in your newsletter. If you have an e-newsletter, ask them to visit your web site to sign up for the newsletter. If you don't ask for and get action from them, your marketing effort was wasted.

Pass out evaluation forms. Afterwards pull out quotes that can be used as testimonials on future seminar invitations. You can always delete words or embellish an idea with the person's permission. When you use the quote on a future invitation, you don't need to use the person's name. Simply identify the person as "CFO of a Fortune 100 company" or "senior partner in an international law firm."

Provide handouts. Every time the prospect comes across the handout that's an exposure to you. For another exposure send an additional page to add to the handout. It is best to wait until the end to distribute the handouts. You don't want the audience to read the handouts instead of listening to you.

Work the room before and after the seminar and at the break, if there is one. Personally introduce yourself to as many people as possible. You may get a piece of information that can and should be worked into your presentation. Even if you don't, the impression you make off-stage is as important as the impression you make on-stage. I go to as many presentations as I can because I like to watch other presenters and I have seen some dead fish. They don't come into the room until they are introduced. When the seminar is over, they stand around looking tired and bored and the message they are sending is, "I wish you all would leave so I can go home." Instead, a successful presenter keeps working the room until the last person has left. The more you interact, the more you become a real person. When that happens, people are much more interested in doing business with you.

FILLING THE SEMINAR ROOM

Now, all of this good advice is for naught if your prep work for the seminar doesn't get people there. So, here are suggestions for filling the room.

1. Invite a lot of people.

Your response rate will vary depending on the topic and the nature of your target market. You should invite more people than you hope will attend. Not everyone you invite will attend and even some of the people who accept will not come.

2. Create marketing materials that market you.

The write-up about you on the invitation should be a marketing piece. If you advertise the seminar, the ad should market you. More people will read your invitation and/or your ad than will attend. Make sure that what they read markets you. I have had many people comment on a seminar I did or a speech I gave, not because they were there, but because they read the invitation or the newspaper write-up. Your invitation should tell the prospect clearly what problem you can solve for him.

3. Send hand-written invitations with a postage stamp.

You don't want to run the risk that your invitation will land unopened in the recycle bin. A hand-written, stamped envelope with a return address has the greatest chance of being opened. We are naturally curious and want to see where we have been invited.

4. Include the agenda.

Include an abbreviated copy of the agenda so they know what will happen, what time it will happen and what kind of information they are going to get. If there is an outside expert, include that person's name and credentials. You are asking for a commitment of time. No one wants to make that commitment without knowing how that time will be spent and without having the answer to the eternal question, WIIFM? When it comes to seminars, people want to be sure that they are not buying the proverbial "pig in a poke."

5. Encourage them to invite a friend.

Encourage them to invite a friend to come to the seminar with them. If they do, it saves you postage, introduces you to a prospect you might not have found on your own and increases the likelihood that the invitee will attend. People usually don't like going someplace where they don't know anyone.

6. Choose the best time and location.

Hold the seminar in a location where your audience is comfortable and at a time of day when they can and want to come. Don't invite women to attend a seminar downtown at night and don't invite business owners to a seminar during the business day.

7. Make it easy to respond.

Include a phone number, an 800 number if you are inviting people who are outside of your local calling area, a fax number, a response card and an e-mail address. Each person has a different preference for the way he wants to respond. The easier you make it to respond, the higher the response rate.

8. Test, test, test.

Don't do everything the same way for the next seminar. Change the time, the location, the topic, but change just one thing with each seminar so that you will know whether or not that change made a difference in enrollment. That's what direct marketers do all the time. In fact, they do split runs. For example, the offer they make in run A would be different than the offer they make in run B. Since that's the only thing they change, they can find out which offer pulled better.

Sometimes the results are surprising. A higher price can end up selling more of a product.

PREPARING FOR THE SEMINAR

A. Seminar Preparation Checklist:

1. Three to four months prior to seminar:

    a. Secure the seminar location.
    b. Choose the seminar topic.
    c. Select a co-presenter, if any.
    d. Design the seminar.
    e. Write first draft of the seminar.
    f. Design the handouts.

2. Two to three months prior to the seminar

    a. If there is a co-presenter, meet with the co-presenter to co-ordinate seminar roles.
    b. Produce handouts.
    c. Produce visuals.
    d. Design invitations.
    e. Develop a prospect list.
    f. Write second draft of the seminar.

3. One month prior to the seminar

    a. Print invitations.
    b. Hand-address envelopes.
    c. Put postage stamps on the envelopes.
    d. Mail invitations.
    e. Write final draft of seminar.
    f. Rehearse. Continue rehearsing every day until the seminar.
    g. Print appointment request cards.
    h. Print evaluation forms.
    i. Acquire notepads and pens.

4. Three weeks prior to the seminar

    a. Confirm seminar arrangements including time, seating, refreshments and audio-visual equipment.
    b. Rehearse with the co-presenter.
    c. Practice using visual aids.
    d. Place first newspaper advertisements, if you are advertising the seminar.

5. Two weeks prior to the seminar

    a. Place second newspaper advertisements.
    b. Fax press release to weekly newspapers.
    c. Call and ask invitees if they will be attending. Encourage them to bring a friend. Ask if they have any questions.

6. One week prior to the seminar

    a. Place third newspaper advertisements.
    b. Fax press release to the daily newspapers.
    c. Have staff person/intern call invitees they could not reach the previous week.
    d. Arrange for back-up audio-visual equipment.
    e. Check out the room you will be using.

7. Two days before the seminar

    a. Call invitees and respondents and tell them that you are looking forward to seeing them.
    b. Re-confirm room arrangements.
    c. Check audio-visual equipment.

8. Morning of the seminar

    a. Finish calls to invitees you were not able to reach.
    b. Again re-confirm the room arrangements.

9. Two hours before seminar

    a. Check seminar room.

b. Place notepads and pens at seats.
c. Set-up check-in table.
d. Retest the audio-visual equipment and the back-up equipment. (Molony's This-Can't-Be-Happening-to-Me Law: If you don't bring back-up equipment, your regular equipment will fail. Always.)

B. Seminar Set-up Checklist:

1. Personal appearance

Presenters and support staff should dress professionally. This may mean a business suit or it may mean business casual depending on your profession. The key word is "professional." Everything is important, from neatly-combed hair to freshly-pressed clothing to polished shoes. Appearance helps project the image of you that you want to project to a room full of prospects and/or their influencers.

In addition, being well-groomed means that the audience will not be distracted by scuffed, run-down shoes, a stained tie or an improperly-buttoned blouse that is gaping open. These things may seem unimportant, but anything that draws attention away from your message or lowers the audience's opinion of you reduces the success of your seminar.

2. Room set-up

Set up fewer chairs than you anticipate needing. It looks better to have to bring in extra chairs than to have empty chairs screaming, "We didn't want to come." Besides, you can expect as much as a one-third fall-off from those who accept to those who attend.

Set up a check-in table that is easy to find, convenient to reach, and out of the line of traffic. This should be manned beginning 45 minutes before the seminar.

Rent or bring your own audio-visual equipment. The equipment should be checked before the seminar and backed-up with spare projector bulbs, white board markers, flip chart pads, markers, erasers and a cordless mike. Play background music during the sign-in process to create a relaxed mood.

Check the quality of the projection surface. Does it set-up properly? Is it large enough? Is it soiled or torn? If so, have it replaced.

Bring these supplies for the audience:

Pads and pens
Information packets
Index cards for questions
Evaluation sheets
Gift for drawing after evaluation sheets have been collected
Handouts for distribution at the end of the seminar

Use support staff:

Have two people at the sign-in table. One of these people will later be in the seminar room while the other one handles late arrivals. At the end of the seminar both will again staff the sign-in table to schedule future appointments.

Seek client testimonials:

If you feel it would be appropriate, ask one or two clients to attend and give testimonials.

C. Seminar Presentation Checklist:

Presenter procedures:
Introduce yourself to people as they arrive.
Maintain eye contact as you talk with them.
Be aware of your posture & gestures.
Be aware of pacing, pitch and vocal variety.
Repeat questions from the audience before you answer them.
Ask the audience to submit questions on index cards. Have an assistant bring up the cards at the end.
Close with a call to action: write—call—send for.
Ask the attendees to fill out the evaluation forms. Collect the forms. Have a drawing for a door prize.
Work the room before the seminar, during breaks and until the last person leaves.

Support staff procedures:
Put notebooks and pads on chairs.
Put index cards for questions on chairs.

Check in all attendees.
Collect question cards during seminar.
Pass out handouts at the end of the seminar.
Pass out evaluation forms at the end of the seminar.
Collect evaluation forms.
Schedule appointments.

D. Post-seminar Checklist:

1. Day after seminar
   a. Mail follow-up materials. Send an additional page to add to the handout.
   b. Call to set-up appointments.
   c. Always follow-up the seminar with a note of appreciation to each attendee. Do this within 48 hours for maximum marketing impact.

If a person could do only one thing to market themselves, I would advise them to write notes to people: thank you notes, congratulation notes, I-read-about-you notes, thought-you-would-like-to-read-this notes, I-heard-something-wonderful-about-you-today notes. The handwritten note is the most powerful marketing tool I know. Writing personal notes is an almost lost art. People receive few of them so those they do receive make an impact. If, by chance, your handwriting is illegible, you could type the note, sign it and, then, add a handwritten post script (P.S.)

A few years ago I read an article about the top salesperson in the insurance industry. He spent the first seven minutes of every day writing notes. Seven minutes is approximately one and one-half percent of the business day. That's all and I am sure that, minute for minute, those were the highest-yielding minutes of his day.

2. Second day after seminar

   a. Finish writing notes of appreciation to each attendee.
   b. Send non-attendees a "seminar highlights" report.

3. One week after seminar

   a. Call the attendees who did not request an appointment at the end of the seminar. Thank them for attending the seminar.

b. Pull quotes from evaluation forms that can be used (with names deleted) as testimonials on future seminar invitations. You can identify the person by title; for example, "COO of a multi-national manufacturing company." Of course, if you know the person well, you could ask for permission to include his name.

c. Debrief the seminar.

Meet with the co-presenter (if there was one), your staff and an external marketing consultant (if you have one) to debrief the seminar and evaluate any questions raised during follow-up calls with attendees.

d. Track results.

1. Track results to find out which newspapers and which dates "pulled" the best.
2. Track results to quantify the new business that comes from the seminar.
3. Track results to identify the referrals that come from the seminar.
4. Track results to document the prospect relationships that develop as a result of the seminar.

e. Initiate a prospect contact program.

The goal of a prospect contact program is to keep the presenter before the prospects so that when they are ready to buy they will think of the presenter. People who responded to the advertisements and invitations, whether they attended the seminar or not, should go into the prospect database and be put on a program of regularly-scheduled contacts by mail and phone.

In addition to the public seminars, you can approach trade associations and professional and civic organizations to do short seminars at their monthly programs. Association databases are available at public and college libraries. Send letters to the groups in your area whose members match your prospect profile and offer your services as a speaker. Follow-up with phone calls. Speaking to membership groups saves you all the big costs associated with doing a seminar. The room rental, the cost of food, the cost of equipment rental and the cost of advertising are handled by the association. All you need to do is provide them with a black and white photo, a bio and a write-up about the seminar for their newsletter. In addition to seeking to be put on their program schedule you can indicate your availability for last-minute fill-in situations when they have a presenter cancel.

E. Private Seminar Checklist:

1. In January:

    a. Contact program directors of selected trade associations and professional and civic organizations. Ask them when their program committee will be planning the program schedule for the coming program year. Usually organizations schedule programs from September to May or June and set their calendar of events in the Spring.
    b. Send interested organizations a cover letter, bio and seminar/speech proposal.

2. When contacted by an organization for a specific speaking date:

    a. Send a program write-up for the organization's newsletter.
    b. Send black and white photo and bio for the organization's newsletter.
    c. Request list of attendees be provided to you after the seminar.

3. Follow the procedures outlined in the above seminar checklists to prepare and present the seminar.

4. Within one week after the presentation:

    a. Send information packets that participants requested.
    b. Call the organization's program director to debrief the program.
    c. Write the organization's program director a thank-you note.

GETTING INTERVIEWED

In addition to speeches and seminars there is another way to use the power of your voice. One of the best ways to increase your visibility and build your credibility is to be interviewed in newspapers, in magazines, in trade journals, in newsletters, on radio and on television.

Many times people are reticent about approaching the media. They think the media couldn't possibly be interested in them. They forget that producers always need guests for their shows and editors always have newspapers and magazines to fill. Publications need paying readers in order to lure advertisers. To get and keep readers the publications have to entertain or educate them. Similarly, radio and television shows need listeners so that the advertisers will pay to advertise on their station. To keep their viewers they have to educate or entertain them.

The media keeps its audience by offering solutions to their problems, whether the problem is boredom or back pain. There is a myth that you have to be a celebrity in order to be interviewed. Don't believe the myth. If I'm bored, I want to be entertained. If I have a backache that won't go away and you write an article about curing a chronic backache, I want to read what you have to say. I don't care if you're famous. I care if you solve my problem.

Getting interviewed on TV or the radio requires the same process that you used to get interviewed by the print media. Study the media outlet. Who is their audience? What problems does the audience have? What do they fear? Can you help them avoid it? What do they want? Can you help them get it? If you can help their audience get what it wants or avoid what it fears, the media outlet might be interested in you.

Of course, they can't call and ask to interview you if they don't know you exist. You have to approach them. You have to get on and stay on the media's radar screens just as you have to always be before your target market. Remember your carefully designed package? It tells the editor/producer what you have done and for whom you have done it. You solve problems. If his audience is comprised of people who have problems you can solve, it is a marriage made in Heaven.

One way of approaching the media is to send press releases. Send the release to the producer of the TV or radio show or the editor of the appropriate section of the newspaper. Do not send your press release to the host of the show.

Popular subjects of press releases are:

1) A special event.
2) A new product or service. (The product does not truly have to be new. It may just be an improved or upgraded product. Think of all the "new" and "improved" detergents.)
3) A free report or booklet or article reprint that you are offering.
4) A new toll-free number.
5) A new Web site.
6) A contest you are sponsoring.

7)   Classes you are offering.

8)   The results of a survey you conducted.

A press release interests an editor or producer if it tells him that what you are about to do will either interest or entertain his readers/viewers. If, and only if, you can provide something his audience wants will he be interested in you and what you are doing. Editors and producers aren't interested in you, per se. They are interested in what you can do for their audience, ie. their target market. So, clearly explain why their readers/viewers would be interested in what you are doing.

When you write your press release, using the proper format for a press release increases the chances that it will be read. Following is a list of style rules which every press release should follow.

PRESS RELEASE STYLE RULES

* Use 8 ½ x 11 inch white paper.
* Leave two inches at the top of the release.
* Use wide margins.
* Double-space the release.
* Write short sentences.
* Write short paragraphs of no more than four or five lines.
* Use action verbs.
* Use active voice. Write "Mr. Morse will make an announcement" instead of "An announcement will be made by Mr Morse."
* Write no more than two pages. One is better.
* Avoid jargon. Instead of "window of opportunity" say, simply, "opportunity."
* Explain technical terms.

A press release must not only follow style rules for its presentation, it must follow organizational rules for its format. Following is the template for a press release.

PRESS RELEASE TEMPLATE

Contact information:

The top line of any press release contains two pieces of information. In the upper right corner write the date of release. It will often say "FOR IMMEDIATE RELEASE, followed by the date." In the upper left corner write the contact name and contact information, including day and evening phone numbers and an e-mail address. Additional contact information is placed at the end of the press release.

Headline:

The headline should be capitalized and centered. The headline is the most important part of any release. It is the only part of the press release that you know will be read. The headline has to make the reader want to keep reading. It is the hook to lure the reporter or editor into the press release. If it doesn't grab him by the throat and make his eyeballs pop, you are probably wasting your time.

Body:

The body of the release has three or four paragraphs. The information appears in order of descending importance. You never know the point at which the reader will stop reading so you need to get the most important information out first. Once again, if this first paragraph doesn't hold the reader's attention, he'll never read the rest.

The beginning of your first paragraph includes the date of the release and the city and state from which it originates. At the end of this paragraph put a hyphen or a series of dashes and begin writing the body of your press release.

The first paragraph answers these questions : Who? What? When? Where? Why? How? These are the standard questions that every newspaper article answers. The second paragraph gives background information about your business and describes your credentials. This information tells why you are The Expert. The third paragraph gives the reader a reason to contact you. You could offer a copy of a free report or booklet. Be sure to tell how the reader can obtain the offered items. This is also where you would provide additional contact information such as telephone number, fax number, and/or e-mail address. Be sure to include an after-hours phone number.

The body of the release follows this format for two reasons. First, the most important information comes at the beginning in case the editor reads only the opening paragraph. Second, if the release has to be cut, the reader will have gotten the most important information.

End:

The end of a press release is indicated by one of two symbols, ### or-30-. The symbol is centered on the page below your final paragraph. If the press release has two pages, center the word "MORE" at the bottom of the first page.

Now let's see a sample press release.

SAMPLE PRESS RELEASE

Resources Unlimited   FOR IMMEDIATE RELEASE
666 Center St.   June 6, 2005
Big Bend, New York 12345
CONTACT: Lee Molony, 1-800-xxx-xxxx
                 xxxxxxx@xxxxxxx.com

A NEW ON-DEMAND SERVICE FOR ENTREPRENEURS

Entrepreneurs know they need to market their businesses, but most cannot afford to put a marketing person on staff. The solution? The Marketing Line.

The Marketing Line is the creation of Lee Molony, President of Resources Unlimited, and author of the new book, *Top Dog*. It is a telephone service that allows business owners to call with their marketing questions and charge the call to Visa or MasterCard. The charge is $50 for a half hour and $95 for an hour and calls are taken between 7 and 10 p.m., Tuesdays and Thursdays.

"Most business owners do not have a background in marketing, " says Molony. "They will tell me, 'I'm good at what I do and marketing isn't it.' In the next breath they almost invariably will add, 'But I know I need to market my business if I want to do more than just survive.'"

Lee Molony has twenty years' experience as a marketing consultant and seminar presenter. She has developed programs for entrepreneurs that help them market their way to sales success. She is a member of the American Marketing Association and The Direct Marketing Association. For additional information, call xyz-xyz-xxxx or e-mail xxxxxxx@xxxxxxx.xxx.

#   #   #

When your press release does its job and the newspaper interviews you or you are interviewed on TV or radio, you will get PR. PR is marketing gold because it is, to quote an old saying, "prayed for, not paid for." It increases your visibility, builds your credibility and creates your desirability.

BUILDING YOUR PRESS KIT

As part of your PR campaign, you will also need to have a press kit. The media are vital to the perception of you as The Expert. You become desirable if your target market reads your words, reads about you, hears you, hears about you and sees you. Without the media much of this won't happen and, if it doesn't happen, becoming Top Dog is far more difficult, if not impossible.

Ralph Waldo Emerson, the 19th century author, essayist, lecturer and philosopher, said, "If you build a better mousetrap, the world will beat a path to your door." Maybe, but probably not. If they don't know you build a better mousetrap, they will never beat a path to your door. That's why you need a press kit.

Your press kit is a promotional package that markets you. It is designed to make people want to talk with you, meet you, interview you. To create a press kit, you will need:

* A folder.

While it is acceptable to use a standard two-pocket folder with a business card cut-out, but it is better to use a folder that is eye-catching. A press kit is worthless if it isn't opened and, if it doesn't grab the recipient's attention, it may go unopened. If you have a folder that has your business logo on it, use that. If you do use a standard folder, select one in a color that is eye-catching. The goal is to make your folder stand out in the pile on the recipient's desk.

* A personalized cover letter.

The purpose of the cover letter is to introduce you to the reader. It should describe your business and give a brief account of your achievements. The purpose of the cover letter is to make the reader curious so that he will read the material in the press kit.

* A biography.

This should be no more than one page and highlight your education and experience. It tells the reader why you are The Expert. Your biography is actually a story about how you have helped solve problems for your clients. The story of your successes is intended to move the media to want to write about you or interview you.

* A list of your honors and awards.

For any honor or award that might be unfamiliar to the reader, explain the criteria that were used in selecting the winner. Also, describe the scope of the competition. Being judged Best of Show in a garden design competition is far more meaningful if the reader knows that you were selected best out of 278 entries.

* A media history.

This includes photocopies of stories written about you, including the name and date of the publication. It also includes a list of your interviews on radio and TV and, for each interview, gives the name of the program, the name of the host, the date the program aired, the station's call letters, the city, the name of the producer and the producer's phone number.

* A photograph.

You should have your picture taken by a professional photographer. The photo should be either a 5" x 7" or 8" x 10" black and white glossy. You could include two photographs, a publicity still taken in the studio and an action shot of you doing what you do professionally. Put a sticker on the back of the photo with your name, address and phone number. Do not write on the back of the photo because the ink may bleed through to the front and destroy the photo. Similarly, write on the sticker before you affix it to the back of the photograph. Otherwise, pressure marks may come through on the front of the photograph.

Constantly update your press kit. As you are published and interviewed, add reprints of your articles and lists of your interviews. Add credits like "a guest on the Kyra Chevalier Show on NBC." This is a good example of leverage. The articles you wrote are now reprints in your press kit. The times you were interviewed are now media credits in your kit. The more interviews you have, the more visible, credible and desirable you become. As you succeed, your press kit grows. As your press kit grows, you succeed. This proves the truth of the old adage, "Nothing succeeds like success." The more quickly you succeed, the sooner your phone will start ringing.

Your press kit and press releases are the hooks you use to get the media's attention and build their interest. Before you can hook them, though, you have to find out who they are. To build a list of media contacts, you could copy names and contact numbers from newspapers and magazines and call television and radio stations to ask for the information. Another way to get contact information is to look in the following books and directories. These resources can be found in college and university libraries or at large public libraries or they may be purchased.

Bacon's Newspaper/Magazine Directory
Bacon's Radio/TV/Cable Directory
Broadcasting and Cable Yearbook
Editor and Publisher International Yearbook
Gale Directory of Publications and Broadcast Media
Matthews Media Directory
Standard Rate and Data Service
Working Press of the Nation

Tip: Try to build relationships with some media contacts. Having a personal relationship greatly increases the chances that you will be interviewed. These relationships will also help you gain access to other people in the media.

Once you have made your media lists, update them regularly. People change jobs all the time. If you want to contact the business editor, call the publication and ask the receptionist for the name of the business editor. Verify the spelling of his name. The editor you worked with in the past may be gone. A press kit sent to the wrong person might be dumped, unread. If you don't care enough to find out their names, they may not care enough to open your press kit.

After you send a press kit, follow-up with a phone call. When you contact a reporter, identify yourself and ask if he has five minutes to talk with you. If he does, tell him that you have several ideas for an article that he might like to consider. Stress how your article will solve a problem that his readers have. If the article won't help his readers, he won't be interested. If he doesn't have time to talk when you call, ask him if he would schedule a phone appointment or if he would like you to mail or fax him an idea sheet.

If he has no interest, ask him for the name of someone else on the paper who might be interested. If he says no one would be, try another reporter in another section of the paper anyway. Maybe that reporter will be interested.

Sometimes you will get lucky and a reporter or producer will call you. What do you do when the call comes in?

1) If you are not available to take the call, return the call as soon as possible.
2) Don't give off-the-cuff answers to questions. If you are surprised by the call, you don't need to answer the reporter's questions immediately. You can ask him about the focus of the interview and arrange a time to call him back.
3) If he is looking for an expert on a topic and that is not your area of expertise, tell him and tell him what your area is. If possible, give him the name of someone who can help him. He will respect your truthfulness and, hopefully, will call you the next time he is looking for someone with your expertise.

PREPARING FOR AN INTERVIEW

Once an interview is scheduled, PREPARE, PREPARE, PREPARE. To prepare for an interview:

1. Study the publication.

What topics have been covered in the past six months? Can you offer new information on one of the topics? What information can you provide that the publication's readers want?

2. Study the show.

Who have their recent guests been? What is the interviewer's style? What is the tone of the show? Serious? Humorous? Can you come across well on this kind of program? Broadcast media presents a problem for you that print media doesn't. The producers want their listeners/viewers to be captivated by you. The worst thing is to have them become bored with you and flip to another channel.

If a producer is interested, he will call you and give you a "trial run." He will ask you some questions and see how you handle yourself. He may be interested in you, but not have a spot right now. If it is a local program, tell him that you would be available as a last-minute fill-in. There are always guests who get sick or have a family emergency or mysteriously just don't show. I attended a meeting where the speaker didn't show. During lunch I watched the program director keep craning his neck toward the door hoping to see the speaker rushing in. He never did. I later found out that the speaker didn't show up because he "forgot." You could be the fill-in speaker for the speaker who forgot.

3. Write a list of probable questions and your answers.

The interviewer may very well not ask those exact questions, but may ask similar questions and you will already have partial answers in mind. As you compose your answers to the questions you may possibly be asked, make sure you are using the answers as a vehicle to get out the information about you that you want the audience to know. Plan what you want your target market to know about you. During the interview, remember your agenda. Even if you are asked questions which do not elicit the information you want to give, you can still find ways to get that information into the answers you give to the questions you are asked.

4. Take a personal write-up.

For a press interview, I type up what I always call " background" information. This includes my biography and all the information I hope will come out in the interview. If the reporter has this information in hand, he will often ask questions based on the information during his interview. Sometimes he will use the information word for word in the resulting article.

Providing this written information also limits a potential problem. The reporter will have the correct spelling of names. He will also have an accurate biography. He will know the correct spelling and meaning of any unusual terms that you use.

5. Prepare a question list for the interviewer.

Ask the interviewer if he would like you to send him a list of possible questions prior to the interview. If he says "Yes," you greatly increase the chance that you will be asked the questions that you want to be asked. He may not use all the questions. He may not even use any of the questions, although that is highly unlikely. Whether he uses all the questions or not, you will have influenced his thinking as he composes his own questions.

MAKING YOUR INTERVIEW A SUCCESS

1. Make your interview memorable.

Make yourself easy to remember by using stories, analogies and statistics. People remember startling statistics. They remember stories. They remember mental pictures. Instead of referring to your dog as "my big dog" or "my German Shepherd," paint a memorable mental picture of the dog. I gave a humorous speech once about my German Shepherd, Brett. I called her "The Dog From Hell." If there were a reform school for dogs, she would have been its star pupil. People who heard the speech still ask me, "How's that bad dog?"

Making your stories easy to remember maximizes their marketing value. People remember the name "Merry Maids" much more easily than "Mary's Housecleaning Service." Their ears will perk up when you say, "My clients have won judgments in personal injury suits that total in excess of fifty million dollars. They won in 97% of their cases." They might very well not notice if you say, "My clients have usually been very successful." We remember "The Dog from Hell" and "fifty million dollars." We don't remember generalities and sound-like-everyone-else names.

2. Present yourself professionally.

Just as with a seminar, it is of utmost importance to be the consummate professional in both conduct and appearance. How you look and speak is as important as what you say. To increase your confidence you may want to join Toastmasters or take a few lessons from a speech coach so that how you say it doesn't detract from what you say.

3. Say "Thank you."

Immediately after the interview send the interviewer a thank-you note. You may even want to send a small gift. A communications coach I know sent a reporter a cookie "tree" after he interviewed her.

Your credibility soars and the perception of you as the expert grows when you get ink or get the camera on you. As you do these things you build the perception of you as the expert. "From the horse's mouth" becomes "From the expert's mouth." You are The Expert. In addition, an appearance on camera is another media credit to add to the list of media credits in your press kit, thus further enhancing your image as The Expert.

PERSONAL MARKETING

The second type of marketing tools that you will use come under the heading of Personal Marketing. Networking and community service are examples of personal marketing. These tools rely on your personal touch. With personal marketing your market sees you in action on an intimate basis.

Networking is an excellent way to meet both prospects and referral sources. You may not belong to the same country clubs as your prospects and their influencers, but you can network with them in community service organizations. You can do volunteer work for the same organizations.

There are obvious places to network and there are less obvious, but equally effective, places. If you are a woman and your target market consists of women who own construction businesses, joining the local chapter of Women in Construction is an obvious networking step. It is less obvious to volunteer to work on an all-woman-constructed Habitat for Humanity house.

When you join organizations, you will receive a membership list. This list becomes part of your prospect database. You may be able to use this list for seminar invitations and for newsletters and other mailings. Before you do, check the organization's rules. Some organizations frown on this. Fortunately, many don't.

There is a process to networking effectively. The process is what makes networking work. As with every other marketing tool, there is a right way to do it and a wrong way. You can spend as much time networking to no avail as you can networking in a way that builds your business.

> In networking it takes the same amount of time, money and effort to do it wrong as it does to do it right. You have to eat a lot of rubber chicken whether you get new business or just indigestion.

Although we often think of networking in terms of networking events, in reality we are networking all the time. A career counselor once said to me, "You are networking every minute that you are out of your pajamas." Actually, your networking can start even before you get dressed in the morning, if you answer the phone or call someone. This means that you are always "on."

NETWORKING NIGHTMARES

Networking can not only be a waste of your time, effort and money, but it can actually "un-market" you. We've all seen instances of this. I've encountered some people that I would put on Networking's Most Wanted List, if there were such a thing.

When I was new to business, I attended a program called, "How to Network." The man presenting the program told the participants that the more business cards you collect at an event, the more successful you have been. I mentally called him The Business Card Bandit. I'd watch him at meetings and see him gleefully leave at the end of the evening with a fistful of business cards. He was delighted, never realizing that he had just wasted some golden opportunities by jumping from person to person in a card-gathering marathon.

Then, there was Roving Rita. When she talked to you, her eyes never stopped roving around the room. She was always looking to make sure that she wasn't missing someone more important than the person to whom she was speaking.

Even worse than Roving Rita was Arrogant Al. I witnessed him in action at a formal networking event. He was talking with a woman when he stopped in mid-sentence and said, "Excuse me. There's someone important that I have to talk to." With that, he turned on his heel and walked away, leaving both me and the woman standing speechless. Sadly, he probably thought that he was "doing it right." He thought he was networking, but what he was actually doing was hanging himself with his own net.

Then, there was Joining Jenna. She was the networking queen or so she was pleased to tell everyone. She bragged that she belonged to 32 organizations. The key to turning membership in an organization into a marketing tool is to be active. You cannot be active in 32 organizations. You cannot be active to the extent needed to have an impact in more than two or three organizations. Being active in an organization allows people to judge your professional ability. If you belong to too many organizations, you are contributing to none or contributing in a haphazard manner. This reflects poorly on your professionalism. The purpose of joining is not just to be seen. It is to be seen and admired. It is far better to join one or two organizations where you can make significant contributions and your talents can shine.

It is not enough to meet a lot of people. You have to meet the right people in the right way and make the right impression. No amount of doing it can make up for not doing it right. You need a networking strategy. Who are the people that you want to meet? What do you know about them? Where can you get more information? Where can you meet them? What groups do they belong to? Can you get access to those groups?

Let's look at where you network. Everywhere. You never know who can help you. In fact, one of the mistakes that people make in networking is to underestimate the value of another person. We know who the "important" people are and we want to network with them. However, the appearance of importance can be deceiving. Sometimes the people who appear important don't have the power network they appear to have, while people who appear unimportant can prove to be powerful contacts.

I heard a story that proves this point. A university was having a conference on women's issues and one of the conference organizers went to the airport to pick up the keynote speaker. The organizer stood at the gate watching for a woman who looked like a keynote speaker, someone wearing a power suit and carrying a briefcase, perhaps a laptop. She stood and watched all the people file out of the plane and couldn't locate her power speaker. She began to think the speaker had missed her flight.

Then, she was approached by a white-haired woman wearing white tennis shoes and carrying a backpack. Definitely not a picture of power, but power can come in unlikely packages. The speaker was so impressed by the conference that she was instrumental in having officials of the university interviewed by the Wall St. Journal and having them receive invitations to appear on major talk shows. Never underestimate the person because of the packaging.

We are always networking. Some great contacts will literally fall into our laps. The others we have to go out and get. It is an expensive, time-consuming process. A networking plan allows you to maximize your investment of time, money and energy.

NETWORKING FOR EFFECT

These are the steps of a successful networking plan:

1. Go where they are.

This sounds elementary, but it's important. Find the organizations to which your target market and their influencers belong. They may be alumni associations, trade associations, professional associations, clubs or special interest groups. Attend their meetings and conferences and trade shows. If you are one of "them," you gain credibility, tearing down the brick wall that is traditionally up between the prospect and the seller.

If there isn't an organization that you can join that serves your target market, you can start one. As the organizer, you have access to everyone in the organization. You have visibility and credibility from day one. Because you are the head of the organization you have a unique marketing advantage.

2. Set goals for each networking event.

Before you go to a networking event, write down your goals. Write down the number of people that you want to talk with. Then, list specific people that you hope will be there. Before the event, research these people. Research them through the media and through other people. Write down the questions you want to ask them and the information you can give them that might help them.

3. Market yourself effectively.

Don't stand and talk with friends. Go out and mingle. Our tendency is to talk to people we know. You won't meet new people that way. If you are shy, help yourself and someone else who is shy by going over and initiating a conversation. At any networking event, you will find one or two people who are shy and don't have the courage to go up and introduce themselves to anyone.

4. Be enthusiastic.

As you talk to people, be enthusiastic. Enthusiasm is contagious. We like and remember people who are enthusiastic. They sparkle.

5. Ask questions and listen to the answers.

This advice is so important that it should have stars around it. Questions are the big door opener. The more questions you ask, the more you learn about the other person. Questions uncover areas of common interest. Whenever I talk about the value of questioning and listening, I am reminded of a story about a young man who went to a dinner party. He sat next to a woman and said nothing, other than asking her questions. At the end of the evening, she commented on what a brilliant conversationalist he had been. In a networking situation, you don't have to wow them. Just let them wow you!

6. Tell stories.

Whenever you can, tell a story. We like stories. We remember stories. We have been weaned on stories since the first caveman kept his family spellbound with the story of his fight with a saber-toothed tiger. A good strategy is to tell a story about one of your clients who had a situation similar to the one you are discussing. Talk about how your work helped the client. A true story helps your listener understand what you do and how your clients benefit.

7. Focus on others.

Focus on helping other people, not just on how they can help you. Perhaps you can give them some information or you may have an article that you think would interest them and you can offer to send it to them. If you are impressed with them, you may offer to pass their name on to someone else. Focusing on how you can help them not only makes you memorable, but it also reduces your networking anxiety. If you concentrate on looking for ways to help others, you will be far less nervous.

8. Keep your word.

Do what you say you will do. If you offer to send an article, send it. If you offer to pass their name on, pass it on. If you say you will call them next week, call them next week. Everything you do markets you and everything you don't do that you say you will do "un-markets" you and can undo all the good you did in a thirty-minute conversation with that person.

People may not remember what you did for them, but they will never forget what you said you would do and didn't. On the other side of the coin, everything you do as a follow-up is another exposure to you. It increases your visibility, builds your credibility and, over time, creates your desirability.

I attended the National Speakers Association convention. I talked to people who wanted to provide professional services to the participants. They rented booths to attract prospects. I discussed my needs and asked them to follow-up with me. Not one of them contacted me. Not one. They wasted both time and money identifying prospects and, then, never contacted them. In contrast, a fellow participant, who was teaching "How To Write and Publish a Book" workshops, did contact me. Lynne Waymon followed-up with me three times even though I wasn't ready to attend one of the workshops. No wonder she went on to write Make Your Contacts Count.

9. Write personal notes.

Write a note to tell each person how much you enjoyed meeting him. Tell him specifically why. Write a note to tell him when you give his name to someone else. If he gave you information that helps you at a later date, write another note telling him how he helped you. Personal notes are rare. I have met countless people at networking functions and received very few follow-up notes. A little note makes a big impression.

In the note remind him of where you met and what you talked about. Notes don't have to be literary masterpieces. They don't have to be works of art. A reporter who had interviewed me lost his job and called me twice for referrals. He sent me two notes that were written in pencil on small yellow index cards. They were not "professional," but what was professional was that he appreciated the two job leads that I sent him enough to thank me for them.

I have spent time with other people, sometimes as long as two hours, advising them and never even gotten a phone thank-you, let alone a written thank-you note. Needless to say, when a job lead comes along that I could pass on to those people, I won't. If you don't care enough to send a thank-you note when someone has gone out of their way for you, I don't consider you a professional and I won't recommend you. The power of the pen cannot be overestimated.

10. Be a friend.

Give any sincere compliment, personal or professional, that you can give. Most people receive far too little praise. We are often criticized and rarely praised.

Congratulate people for their achievements. When you read about someone in a newspaper or magazine, send him a congratulatory note or card and include a copy of the article. If you have heard someone praised, tell him. We all like to know when other people are giving us good word-of-mouth advertising.

Send people in your network cards and notes and tips and leads and articles. Relationships need "watering" just as plants do. Take every opportunity to show people you like them and want to help them. Maintain relationships even if they do not seem to be helping you build your business. The person who can't hire you today may refer you tomorrow and hire you two years from now.

If you can comfortably refer someone, do it. At this point I have to issue a word of warning: Be cautious about giving referrals. I am very careful when I give a referral. When I do, I am endorsing the person being referred and don't want it to ever come back and haunt me. If I haven't worked with the person myself, I will give a qualified referral. If I have heard good things about the person, I will say, "I haven't worked with this person. I cannot speak from experience, but I have been told that he is good." That way, if he isn't a first-rate attorney or dentist or graphic artist, it won't come back to haunt me.

10. Build a database of all your networking contacts.

Write down the basic biographical and business information. Make short notes on what you discussed each time you met. If you have something in common, note that. If you gave or were given referrals, note that. If you promised to do something, note that. When you do what you promised to do, note it. You may think you will remember the conversation and your follow-up, but we cannot possibly remember everything we say, everything we do, everything someone else says and everything someone else does. To construct your database you can either write contact sheets that you keep in a notebook or you can use a computer contact manager. The choice is yours. The choice of paper notebook or contact manager ultimately doesn't matter. What does matter is that you have and use a system that contains complete contact information. A system you aren't comfortable with is a system you won't use. A system that you don't use faithfully is worthless. Regardless of your system choice, keep a back-up. If you lose all your contact information, you will have lost information you can never regain and you may have lost your best chance of finding a new job, should you ever want one.

You need a plan for networking just as you need a plan for every other facet of your marketing strategy. Work your plan. Do everything on purpose. If you have a plan and diligently follow it, networking is a fantastic marketing tool. If you don't, your investment of time, energy and money may be wasted.

CHAPTER FIVE

APPROACHING YOUR MARKET

So far you have:

Looked at potential target markets.
Selected your target market.
Profiled your target market.
Introduced yourself to your target market.

Now you are ready for Part Five of TDS, the Top Dog System. Part Five is Approaching Your Market or, in Top Dog terms, *Entering the Show Ring*. Before you can approach them, however, you have to find individual qualified prospects. What is a qualified prospect? A qualified prospect is anyone who says or does something that indicates that he is interested in what you offer.

If you don't buy lists, where can you find bona fide prospects in your market? You can join trade associations and get their membership lists. You can find the name of national trade associations by going online to one of the popular search engines and typing in "Trade Associations." The search will lead you to the trade associations in various industries.

Getting membership lists from trade associations is not the only way to build your prospect list. If you do business-to-business marketing, another way to build your personal list of prospect names is to subscribe to Hoover's Online. If your target market is CEO's of manufacturing companies in the tooling and machining industry, you will find their names along with the profiles of their companies.

Traditionally, prospecting has put the emphasis on getting lists of names of people to contact. That's what we have been talking about. There is another prospecting strategy that is even better. This strategy is to get the prospects to tell you who they are. For example, if you are a veterinarian, you could approach the local Humane Society and offer to teach a free class in how to keep your new pet healthy. The people who sign up for the class become your qualified prospects. If you do decorative painting in people's homes, you could give a free demonstration at a home store. After the demonstration the people who sign a list to make an appointment for a free estimate become your qualified prospects. If you are a chiropractor and are interviewed on TV, the people who send for your free booklet on exercises to reduce back pain become your qualified prospects.

When you compile a list from organizations and associations, the people on it are prospects because they fit the profile of your target market. However, they may or may not turn out to be qualified prospects. A qualified prospect is one who says, "I want what you do." The prospects who send for the chiropractor's free booklet are qualified prospects. They have said, "I am interested in what you offer."

APPROACHING YOUR PROSPECTS

Once you find bona fide prospects, you are ready to approach them and say, "Look at me! Look at me! I can help you." A word of caution: In Part Five you are not selling. Prospecting isn't selling. Prospecting is marketing. Only one part of the Top Dog System, the sales call, is selling. Everything else is marketing.

So, if prospecting is not selling, why is prospecting so difficult that many of us can find countless tasks that have to be done before we can pick up the phone? There's a one-word answer. Rejection. REJECTION. REJECTION! REJECTION!!

The fear of rejection has kept more people from becoming Top Dog than any other factor. It is a more important factor than age, gender, race, religion, nationality, physical disabilities, education, experience or the economy. Your biggest enemy is fear, both your fear and your prospect's fear. No one wants to be rejected. You know if you don't make the call you can't get shot down. The prospect is afraid, too. He is afraid of making a mistake. He is afraid of making his life worse.

He puts up a brick wall between himself and you because of his fear of you. Put yourself in his shoes. He is afraid you could harm him. Even if he isn't happy with your competitor's service at least he feels safe. As the old saying goes, "Better the devil you know than the one you don't." You have to overcome the barrier created by fear. It is Newton's First Law again. A body at rest will stay at rest unless acted upon by an outside force. You are that force.

Before you can overcome the barrier the prospect has erected between the two of you, you have to get around the barrier you have erected inside your own head. This barrier prevents you from approaching the prospect in the first place. This barrier is created by your fear of rejection.

We all fear hearing the dreaded word, "No." It isn't hearing "No" that destroys you, though. It's letting the "no" upset you mentally and physically that destroys you. A fisherman doesn't become upset if the fish don't bite. He just keeps fishing. He certainly doesn't take it personally if they don't.

Prospecting should be like fishing. Visualize the prospects out in the middle of the lake drowning. You are rowing out to save them. Keep telling all the drowning people you can save them until you find the ones who want to be saved. Some don't want to be saved or don't want to be saved by you. Just keep rowing. Just keep fishing. Eventually the fish will bite. Eventually you will find the prospects who want you to save them.

The salesperson who takes rejection personally avoids the behaviors that caused him to feel pain. If rejection caused no pain, you would keep on trying. The scientist, B. F. Skinner, in explaining his Theory of Operant Conditioning, showed that if a rat is put in a cage and there is a lever for food, the rat will push the lever simply because it is there. Once he presses the lever and gets food, he will continue to press it. Who wouldn't? Surprisingly, he will push the lever the longest when he doesn't get food every time. Since there is no pattern, the rat keeps trying. It will take a long time before he gives up. After all, next time the food pellet might come out. The most powerful reinforcement is intermittent reinforcement.

It's the same with prospecting. If you take the pain out and keep asking, sometime the prospect will say, "Yes." You are encouraged to keep trying because "sometime" may be the next time. Intermittent reinforcement allows you to say, "I don't know when I will get a prospect, but I know that sooner or later I will." "Sometime" it will happen.

Intermittent reinforcement is actually better than positive reinforcement. If the rat got the pellet every time he pushed the lever, the first time the pellet didn't drop, he would decide the lever no longer worked and stop pushing. The prospects who say "yes" provide intermittent reinforcement. All the prospects who say "no" are simply the fish that don't bite. Stay in there until you get to the occasional prospect who says "yes." You never know when you will find that prospect so you are encouraged to keep trying. "Sometime" is always just around the corner so there is no reason to quit. "Sometime" might be the next push of the lever.

Prospecting is a numbers game. Pure and simple. It hurts only if you think emotionally rather than strategically. Thinking strategically allows you to feel that you weren't rejected. The lever just didn't drop a pellet this time. "Sometime" will come, maybe even with the prospect who just said, "No." "Sometime" always comes.

For your emotional health, learn to love hearing the word "no." Babe Ruth heard "Strike three. You're out!" more than any other batter. That's because he was up to bat enough times to hit 60 home runs. His record stood for 34 years. If you aren't willing to strike out, you will never go up to bat. If you don't get up to bat, you can't hit a home run. It's that simple.

A strike is a strike. A "no" is a "no." A "no" isn't a value judgment. A "no" simply means "I don't want to be saved." When a prospect says, "I don't want to be saved," he may really mean, "I don't want to be saved now. Row your boat out to me later." On the other hand, he may never want you to "save" him. Either way, it is just a strike, not a failure.

You may never know the real reason you are rejected. The prospect may never know the real reason he is rejecting you. So don't waste your time on psychoanalysis. Pick up the phone and move on.

This is not to say that how you ask isn't important. It is VERY important and we'll talk about that later. Right now, my main objective is to show you how to move from REJECTION, The Bottomless Pit of The Damned, onto safe ground, The Home of Top Dog. Do you think Top Dog is cowering in the corner, dreading the next kick? No, Sir. He is asking, giving himself a check for every time he asks, knowing that after so many asks he will, as surely as the sun comes up in the East, get a "Yes." In fact, he has probably reached the enviable position where he isn't asking at all. He is being asked. You will get there, too.

First, realize that rejection isn't personal. In most cases the people you prospect don't know you. They are not "out to get you." You just happen to cross their path at a time when they don't want what you are offering. In fact, they may not want anything except to get out of their own skin.

There is also an unfortunate phenomenon that I had explained to me when I first went into business. Susan had worked for several major companies selling support for large computer installations. At thirty-two she was a battle-hardened warrior. She said to me, "Perfectly nice people will be nasty to vendors. It's okay in their book because you are just a salesperson." Of course, not everyone will do that, but there is an element of truth to what she said. They may be having a bad day. They may have just had a bad week. They may be having a bad life. You call and it is perfectly safe to let go on you.

How your market perceives you will have a great impact on your success. Are you "just a salesperson?" Look at how the public perception of the stockbroker has changed in the past thirty years. First they were stockbrokers. They were, in essence, people who took buy and sell orders. Then, they became account executives. Now they are financial consultants or advisors. Their clients are no longer buying stocks and bonds. They are buying advice and planning and a relationship. As the industry moves more and more toward a financial-planning, fee-based business, the financial consultant has come to be perceived as an advisor, not as a salesperson.

HANDLING REJECTION

Even knowing that you need to hear all those "no's" before you get to a "yes," doesn't mean the process will be easy. It won't be. It will just be easier than it would have been if you had taken it all personally. To make the process as easy as possible, try these coping strategies.

1. Don't take it personally.

They don't even know you so they aren't out to get you.

When we call someone, we aren't working with a blank slate. That person has a lifetime of experiences and a cauldron of emotions that we are stepping into. Maybe they have just received bad news. Maybe they have had a bad experience in the past. Maybe they have a prejudice against women or a certain race or ethnic group or against doing business with someone who is younger than they are or older. Maybe you remind them of someone they don't like, their mother-in-law, brother, their high school geometry teacher (mine was Attila the Hun) or their former husband or wife. It's not your fault that you remind them of someone they dislike. Don't take it personally.

2. See yourself through their eyes.

We know we have something valuable that can help our prospects, but, when we call them, they don't see someone who can help them. They see an interruption, possibly an annoyance. They also see risk. You could hurt them. Down at the gut level, below all the reasons that the prospect would give if you asked him why he didn't want to meet with you, down at the gut level is fear. The prospect is afraid of what you could do to him. He may not be happy where he is, but he could be a lot worse off. This fear has to be added into the equation. He may be having a bad day, possibly a bad life. He doesn't have the time to talk with you and, even if he did, he doesn't need any more aggravation.

Put yourself in your prospect's shoes. There are an incredible number of things going on emotionally and physically in that person's life. If you were that person, you wouldn't want to talk to you either. See yourself through his eyes.

3. Play the numbers.

It's a numbers game. Fill in this formula:

x calls = y appointments = z sales

You have to make x calls to get y appointments and keep y appointments to close z sales.

Your numbers may be 100 calls to get ten appointments to close five sales. Your numbers may be 200 calls to get ten appointments to close two sales. If you are just starting your business, the equation could be 600 calls to get ten appointments to close one sale. Whatever your numbers are, you have to make that number of calls for each sale you want to make. You can't escape the numbers. Of course, your x will be a smaller number the longer you are in business. You will need to make fewer calls to get appointments and need fewer appointments to close a sale. At some point you may make 15 calls to get five appointments to close one sale or five calls to get three appointments to close one sale.

No matter how long you are in business, though, you are always working your equation. There are a certain number of calls you have to make. Let's go back to our first set of numbers. If you make 100 calls and get 10 appointments, 90 people said, "No." If this is your equation, you know 90 people will say "No" out of every 100 you call. So, there is no need to feel rejected. It's a numbers game. Just keep calling because the sooner you get the 90 "No's" out of the way, the sooner you'll get to the 10 "Yes's" that will ultimately yield one sale.

4. Focus on behavior, not results.

This is difficult when you start in business. You may have management looking at results. Even if you don't have management looking at the results and holding you accountable, you will be looking and holding yourself accountable.

This is exactly the opposite of what you should do to fight the demon of rejection. You can't control whether or not someone buys from you. If your focus is on how many people hang up on you or on how many people don't buy from you, it is difficult not to let rejection eat at you and do terrible things to your head and your heart and your digestion.

Instead, focus on your actions. Your actions are the only things you can control. How many calls did you make? How many sales letters did you send out? How many seminars did you do? How much business work did you do that could produce results (i.e. going on sales calls, calling clients, practicing speeches, writing articles) as opposed to how much busy work (i.e. reading the paper, getting a cup of coffee, going to the bank) that can't produce results? Focus on your behavior. Winners hit more home runs than other players. Winners also strike out more than other players. The strike-outs are just part of being up at bat enough times to get the opportunity to hit a lot of home runs. Of course, each call, each time at bat has to be a quality, 100% effort. Half-hearted efforts don't count. Your effort doesn't count if it is the marketing equivalent of the adolescent who showed up at my door holding out a fund-raising calendar and saying, "You don't want to buy one of these, do you?"

5. Welcome the word, "No."

The people who say "No" are doing you a favor. They are keeping you from wasting your time and energy trying to ride a dead horse. The faster they say "No," the sooner you get to the prospects who say, "Yes." Love all the "no's" that get you there. If you welcome the word rather than fearing it, being rejected becomes merely the cost of doing business, not a devastating blow.

6. Change your picture of yourself.

You are not a beggar asking for a crumb. You aren't asking people to do you a favor and give you an appointment. You are asking them to give you an appointment so you can help them get what they want. In fact, you are doing them a favor. You are asking to help them, just as a doctor helps a patient. Changing your picture of yourself will change the image that other people have of you.

7. Know the odds.

It's a fact that, if the prospect has an existing relationship, the odds are not in your favor. It's easier for the person to keep doing what he has been doing than to do something new. Laziness is a factor. Fear is another factor. You can take the sting out of this situation by remembering that, while the odds are against you in trying to woo away someone else's clients, they are with you in keeping the clients you have. In the end, that is the most important thing that you can do.

Conclusion:

Using these seven coping strategies can help you handle rejection and keep it from handing you defeat. How you handle rejection plays a huge part in how successful you will ultimately be. If you can control your emotional reactions, you will eliminate the biggest reason for failure. You can't hang in there until you succeed if you let your reactions to all those "No's" hang you.

Rejection doesn't matter. Our response to it does. If we respond with anger or sadness or frustration or a feeling of hopelessness, we put burdens on ourselves that don't have to be there. The greatest barriers to our success are not external barriers. They are not what people say or do. They are the barriers in our head. If we let rejection get to us, we put up more roadblocks than anyone else could ever erect against us.

Once you have mastered your ability to handle rejection you will be able to consistently and persistently prospect. If you persist, you will be successful. Period. Keeping in contact with both clients and prospects regularly is like panning for gold. You do it and do it and do it. If you quit after the first week or month or year, you leave the gold behind for someone else to find. You have to keep prospecting and prospecting and prospecting.

Perseverance means calling prospects, year after year.
Perseverance means sending sales letters, year after year.
Perseverance means doing seminars, year after year.
Perseverance means giving speeches, year after year.
Perseverance means writing for publication, year after year.
Perseverance means mailing press kits, year after year.
Perseverance means joining groups and working in them, year after year.

Conditions change and the prospect who was not interested yesterday may be interested today. The prospect who was not qualified last year may be qualified this year. The prospect who didn't want your services last year may need your services this year. The prospect who was pleased with their current provider last year may be angry as a wet hen this year and looking to change. If you're not calling regularly, when he changes it won't be to you.

The majority of salespeople stop calling too soon. The Dartnell Corporation and McGraw-Hill both did studies that yielded similar results. They found that 80% of all sales are made after five or more contacts.

80% of all sales are made after the 5th call.
48% of salespeople quit after one call.
25% quit after two calls.
12% quit after three calls.
Only 15% persevere beyond three calls.

That means that 85% of your competition is gone by the time you make the fourth call. You will have virtually no competition left by the fifth call when 80% of sales are made. In the end 10% of all salespeople make 80% of all sales. Extremely successful salespeople ask more people and ask them more times. Babe Ruth was home run king. He was also strike-out king. If you aren't willing to get up to bat again and again and again, you can't hit home runs again and again and again.

But swinging often is not enough. You need a step-by-step action plan. An action plan consists of measurable goals to be reached in a specified period of time. For example, your ultimate goal may be to earn $150,000 this year. This goal can be achieved only by meeting yearly, monthly, weekly and daily goals. A yearly goal might be to make 1250 new prospect calls, to send 500 personal notes, to make 500 prospect relationship calls to prospects that you are cultivating, to make 500 client relationship calls, to send 750 sales letters, to do twelve seminars and to submit four articles for publication.

Achieving these goals is easier if you make timelines for the tasks you need to accomplish in order to produce seminars, speeches and articles for publication. If you want to achieve your yearly goal of submitting four articles for publication, your timeline might look like this.

1) Complete the research for the first article by _____.
2) Select the publication to approach by _____.
3) Submit query letter by _____.
4) Outline the article by _____.
5) Write the first draft by _____.
6) Make revisions by _____.
7) Have the article proofread by _____.
8) Mail the article to the publication by _____.

Then, do this for the second, third and fourth articles that you want to have published during the year.

The easiest way to achieve your yearly goal is to break it down into monthly, weekly and daily goals for every marketing task. To reach your yearly goal, your daily goals would be:

To make five new prospect calls.
To make two prospect relationship calls.
To make two client relationship calls.
To send two notes.
To send three sales letters.
To work on seminars for one hour.
To work on articles for publication for thirty minutes.

I don't know about you, but I know I absolutely have to set daily goals. I do poorly if I have only weekly or monthly goals. If my weekly goal is twenty sales letters, it is easy for me to keep pushing that task ahead a day. After all, there is always Friday. Then, what happens? You know. Friday comes and an emergency rears its ugly head or I'm tired or sick or have Spring fever or am on overload. I look at my weekly task list, see that I still need to send out twenty sales letters and think, "You've got to be kidding!" Then, this week's goal of twenty sales letters becomes next week's goal of forty sales letters and a bottle of Excedrin. I don't do well with weekly goals. I can handle daily goals pretty well. At least it is a lot harder to fool myself if I'm not on target.

Having a timeline and monitoring your daily tasks in order to stay on track for meeting your yearly goals gives you the best chance of meeting your ultimate goal of earning $150,000 this year. You may still fall short, but your chance of meeting your ultimate goal is far greater if you set your yearly goal and your chance of meeting your yearly goal is greater if you set and meet your monthly, weekly and daily goals. If you don't, you will always be in "Gonna Land." "I'm gonna" won't get you where you want to go.

Goals provide a way to measure your success. They measure the activity needed to generate action. They also provide motivation. People who set goals and then work to achieve them have higher incomes and less stressful lives.

The action steps needed to achieve a goal are measurable. You either mailed three sales letters on Thursday or you didn't. You either made five cold calls on Monday or you didn't. By completing each of the steps on schedule you will reach your goal.

There are two things to note about this process. First, say "I do," "I mail," and "I call," not "I will do," "I will mail," and "I will call." "I will" tells your brain that you don't have to do it today. Tomorrow or next week or next month will be fine. Our brains work only on the command, "Now." "Do this. Now."

The second thing to note is that the weekly, monthly and yearly goals you set must be realistic. A daily goal of making forty phone calls and writing an entire article for publication is unrealistic because it can't be done. The numbers you choose have to be achievable.

Selling is a numbers game. Marketing should be a numbers game, too, not a nebulous activity you "should do." If I had ten dollars for every business owner who has told me, "I know I need to market, but….," I'd be on a beach in the Caribbean right now. To know your marketing numbers, chart the number of marketing activities you engage in daily, weekly, monthly, yearly. The number of sales letters you send. The number of networking events you attend. The number of committees you serve on. The number of personal notes you send. The number of speeches you give. The number of seminars you do. The number of articles you write. The number of press releases and press kits you mail. The number of letters to the editor you write. The number of trade shows you attend. The number of requests for referrals you make. The number of testimonials you seek. The number of times you say, "Look at me!" If you don't know your numbers, you either don't have a marketing plan or you have a plan and aren't working it. Either way it is a certain indicator of future failure.

A marketing action plan keeps you on target. With a plan you know what you need to do and you know if you are doing it. If you are meeting the daily and weekly goals you have set in your plan, your business will be a success.

PSYCHOLOGY OF THE SALE

Persistence is the most accurate indicator of ultimate success. Being persistent isn't easy, though. While you are doing your marketing activities and checking them off, you still have to contend with the other side of the equation, the prospect. On one side you have your passion, your process and your persistence. On the other side of the equation you have the prospect. We have talked about all the reasons why prospects don't want to talk to you. There are many, but there is always one reason why they will want to talk to you. People always want to talk to The Expert.

Now how does someone new to your industry become the expert? You do it not by presenting yourself as the expert in a product or service. That is a given. You present yourself as the best person to fulfill a need: the elderly widows' financial advisor or the tool & die industry's marketing consultant or the legal advisor to Asian business owners.

Presenting yourself as The Expert is only the first step, though. You next have to create a belief in your market that you are, indeed, The Expert. One of the best ways to do this is to educate your target market. The person who is educating the market is automatically viewed as an expert. What you tell your prospects and clients may be something that every other dentist or financial consultant or doctor or accountant or lawyer or chiropractor or architect or physical therapist or nurse practitioner in town knows. That doesn't matter. What matters is that you are the one providing the education.

Fundamental to presenting yourself as The Expert is to project an aura of quiet confidence. As part of the mental game you have to play in order to defeat feelings of rejection and project confidence, put the "power of positive thinking" into perspective. Grab it, wrestle it to the ground and stare at it long and hard. Positive thinking is great, but it is not the answer to all your problems. In fact, it can cause some of them. Positive thinking can cause stress. I remember working with a client who said to me, "I won't tolerate anyone around me who doesn't think positively all the time." That attitude didn't seem wise or realistic to me.

First of all, no one is positive all the time. Second, positive thinking has some drawbacks. It is a fantastic motivator. At the same time, though, it can lead you to beat yourself up with statements like, "I'm not doing it right. I can't sell. I'm a failure." When you think positively and it doesn't work, it is natural to assume that all you have to do is think more positively and work harder. What you really need to do is work smarter. If you are working hard and failing, your process isn't working. Change your process and your positive thinking will give you the extra lift you need to persevere. If you are doing it wrong, no amount of doing or positive thinking will make it right.

It is like trying to knock down a locked steel door by running into it with your shoulder. Running harder or faster or more often or for a longer time still won't open the door. All it will do is damage your shoulder (and your ego!) more. What you need is a key to unlock the door or a battering ram or a way to get around the door or over the door or under the door. Change your process. Positive thinking alone never opened a door. But, positive thinking and the right process will always open the door because positive thinking will help you stay in there until you generate the numbers you need to open enough doors.

Constantly and consistently work your process. You can't get a "Yes" if you don't ask. Get off the wall. Have you ever been to a middle school dance? The boys are holding up the wall on one side of the gym and the girls are holding up the wall on the other side of the gym. In fact, in the past the girls who weren't asked to dance were called "wallflowers." The problem was that nobody did what they came to do. Just scoping out the prospects isn't enough.

Instead, ask and ask and ask. Eventually, you'll get a rhythm. Seven asks, one yes. Seven times at bat, one home run. You're not rejected the six times you strike out. It's all part of a process. You're just striking out six times to get to your seventh time at bat, your home run.

To help you keep rejection at bay, take a piece of paper. Make two columns, one labeled "Calls" and the other one labeled "Qualified Prospects." Every time you contact a prospect put a "C" in a box in the Call column. They don't have to say, "Yes." All you have to do is step up to the plate and swing at the ball. When you do get a positive response (a request for more information, a request for a call back at a specified time, an appointment), put a "P" in the Qualified Prospects column.

Calls	C	C	C	C	C	C	C
QP		P					P

At the end of the month, add up your C's and your P's. Divide the total number of C's by the total number of P's. That shows, on average, how many times you have to pull the lever, get up to bat, make the call, ask the prospect, in order to create a qualified prospect. A qualified prospect is a prospect who says, "I am interested." The C's are times at bat. The P's are home runs. How many times do you have to step up to the plate (ask) to get a home run (qualified prospect)? You are measuring and giving yourself credit for your actions, not for the results. You can control your actions. You can't control the results.

Count what is in your control, not what is outside of your control. You have no control over how many people say, "Yes." You have complete control over how many people you ask.

To keep yourself on track, everything you do should be done on purpose and on task. On purpose means that every action you take is done as part of an overall plan. On task means that every action you do is measurable and is being measured.

How much income do you want to produce this year?
How many sales must you make to generate that income?
How many sales calls do you have to go on to get one sale?
How many prospecting calls do you have to make to get one sales call?

It is a numbers game. The number of prospecting calls. The number of appointments/sales calls. The number of sales. These numbers are determined by the number of:

calls you make.

sales letters you send.

requests for referrals you make.

requests for testimonial letters you make.

prospect contacts you make.

client contacts you make.

influencer contacts you make.

networking events you attend.

articles you submit.

speeches you give.

seminars you do.

interviews you seek.

books you write.

The number of marketing activities you do <u>directly</u> affects the number of sales you make. If you failed to make your sales quota, you failed because you didn't do the required number of activities specified in your marketing plan. It is a numbers game.

WORKING YOUR PLAN

As with anything in life, there is a right way and a wrong way. The wrong way isn't always wrong because it doesn't work. It may be wrong because, even though it works, it takes too long and costs too much for the results you achieve. Jonas Gadson is a motivational speaker. He is intense and uses wonderful stories and analogies to make his points. One analogy that he uses explains the difference between doing it and doing it right. Jonas used to have a long driveway and drove a BIG boat of an automobile. You could have parked a mobile home in Jonas' car. In the Winter, he had to shoot out of his driveway because at its base the driveway dipped and, if he didn't generate enough momentum and just keep going, the car would have come to a stop and Jonas would have been sitting in his driveway until Spring with the tires spinning and spinning and spinning, generating a lot of activity but no action. You want action, not just a flurry of activity. With activity, you look productive. With action, you are productive.

Process in sales means creating and working a business-generating machine. Hard work won't pay if you are doing the wrong things. Process means that each action you take is planned. Each action leads to the bottom line, a 100% referral-based business. There are no random activities, no spinning wheels. You have to create a process and follow it. The process creates sales, which create cross-selling and upselling. The process also generates referrals which create more sales which create more cross-selling and upselling and generate more referrals. If you passionately persevere in following a process, you will move from where you are now to where you want to be, an extremely successful professional with a 100% referral-based business.

SURVIVAL TACTICS

Up until this point you have been getting ready for battle. You have:

- Defined the product.
- Selected a target market.
- Discovered what needs you can fill.
- Identified prospects in your market.
- Planned and implemented your marketing strategy in order to build visibility, credibility and desirability.

Now you are ready to gird your loins and begin prospecting. Prospecting means calling and writing your target market in order to get appointments. At this point, you are still not selling. You are marketing to facilitate the sale. The goal is a 100% referral-based business with a high percentage of long-term clients. The sooner you build your reputation as The Expert, the sooner people will be calling you to ask to do business with you. You aren't there yet, though. So, while you are sowing the seeds of future success, you have to get over the current hurdle, survival. As part of your sales plan, you will be engaging in two survival activities. These activities are cold-calling and sending sales letters to prospects. The more marketing you do, the sooner you can move away from these activities, but initially survival is the name of the game.

Cold calling is not fun. Cold calling is brutal. You are that interruption, that irritation, that annoyance on the other end of the line. So let's see how to quickly turn those cold calls into warm calls. "Quickly" is the operative word because you have only a few seconds to do it before the prospect hangs up. Your pitch has to be pure marketing. The emphasis needs to be on what you can do for them. Your goal is to get face-to-face. No one is going to give up time, which equals money, to meet with someone unless they think they could gain more than they lose in work not done. You have only a few seconds to market yourself to an appointment.

Sadly, most cold calls are a complete waste of time. Think of the cold calls you have gotten. They usually follow one of two scripts.

Script A:
"Hello, I'm James Smith with Fiddle, Dee & Dee. How are you today?"

What does he care?! Besides, if the caller mispronounces your name and asks you how you are, you know immediately that he wants to sell you something you don't want.

Script B:
"Hello, I'm Betty Chamberlain with Fee, Fi, Fo & Fum. How are you? I'm calling some people in your neighborhood today."

Isn't that nice? Click.

Tip: When you cold call, remember:
Thou shalt not say, "I'm calling people in your neighborhood today."
Thou shalt not ask, "How are you today?"

Compare those openers with this one:

"Hello, Ms. Molony. I'm Betty Chamberlain with Fee, Fi, Fo & Fum. I specialize in helping women business owners build a personal nest egg."

I know Betty wants to sell me something, but I may not immediately hang up on her because she quickly told me that she specializes in me. She told me that she can help me solve a problem. She changed the call from a cold call to a slightly warm call. Here is an even stronger opener for a cold call:

"Hello, Ms. Molony. Kelly Winter suggested I call you. I am Betty Chamberlain with Fee, Fi, Fo & Fum. I specialize in helping women business owners build personal nest eggs. Is this an area of concern for you?"

Am I interested in what Betty Chamberlain has to say? I don't know, but I'll listen if Kelly Winter is either a friend or a business associate that I respect. By referring to Kelly Winter Betty Chamberlain made this an even warmer call.

Prospects are resistant to cold calls. Everyone is. Think of how you react when someone you don't know calls you. We are overwhelmed by unsolicited calls. They make us angry. That's why you need a hook. Kelly Winter's name was the hook Betty Chamberlain used.

If you can't open with a personal referral as Betty Chamberlain did, open with a sentence that says, "I know where you hurt." For example, if you are a marketing consultant, you could open with, "I have an idea that my clients have found helps them to increase customer retention by 37%." This hits home. The cost of lost customers is high. It hurts. Keeping more of them is the benefit that you offer. Always lead with your benefit. The opener should arouse curiosity and a tell-me-more response. Don't tell too much, though. Even though you have their attention, they are still looking for a reason to not talk to you and most definitely to not meet with you. Your goal is to get a face-to-face meeting so don't tell so much that they learn all they need to know from talking with you and, thus, have no need to meet with you.

The benefit offered should be focused on the reduction of pain. We want to address the prospect's pain because it is a fact of human nature that we will do more to avoid pain than we will to get pleasure. The stronger the discomfort the prospect feels, the more he wants to relieve the discomfort. Pleasure is having happy employees. Pain is employee turnover with the consequent wasted cost of training. Training costs hurt. However, for you to successfully persuade your prospect to meet with you, the pain has to be strong. It has to reach the level in his mind where he wants to take action.

When Betty Chamberlain called me, she talked about helping me build a personal nest egg. This concern is already in my mind. I worry about having sufficient personal assets that are separate from my business. I think about what assets I would have left if the business fails or I close it to go raise yaks in Montana. The possibility of not having what I need to have is the pain. All Betty Chamberlain has to do is make me feel the pain.

This strategy works for a call-back, too. If you are calling a prospect for the second time, immediately bring back the pain you identified in your first call. Say something like, "The last time we spoke, you were worried about _____. Are you still concerned about _____?"

Write your opener and rehearse it until it sounds natural. Betty Chamberlain planned her opening sentences so that she would grab my attention, stop me from hanging up and remind me of my fear of possibly losing my assets. Her goal was to make relieving the pain a priority so that I would take time I don't have to meet with someone I don't know.

After you write and rehearse your opener, write and rehearse the rest of your call. Winging it won't work. Know exactly how you are going to present the benefit that you are offering.

If I were willing to continue the conversation with Betty Chamberlain beyond the opener, she could say, "I have worked with one hundred and twenty women business owners. My reason for calling you is to share an idea with you that they have used to grow their personal assets an average of 42%. Would you be willing to meet with me for 20 minutes to see if the idea could help you, too?" Will I gave her 20 minutes? If my fear is strong enough, I will.

As with every other aspect of your marketing you need to have a strategy for your cold calls. The most successful cold calls follow the strategy that Betty Chamberlain used. These are the steps:

1) Make an opening statement that grabs their attention. Then, listen.

2) Ask a question that probes for their pain. Then, listen.

3) Make a statement that paraphrases what the prospect said to make sure you understood it and to grow their pain. Then, listen.

4) Suggest a solution that your clients have found helpful. Then, listen.

5) Ask for an appointment.

If you find that they have a problem you can solve, but they are already working with someone, exit gracefully, but leave the door open for the future. Ask if you could, from time to time, send them some literature that might help them. Ask if you could send them your newsletter. If you can, take the opportunity to do some market research. Ask, "What is it you like about working with _____? Is there anything you don't like about working with _____?" The answers to these questions provide invaluable competitor intelligence.

Every prospect you call has one question uppermost in his mind: "What's in it for me?" That's why you have to <u>immediately</u> talk about the benefit you can offer them. I suggest that my clients write this question on a big sign and tape it up next to their telephone. That's the question your prospects are asking themselves. That's the question you have to answer immediately. Always think "WIIFM?"

You are a vendor. Your goal is to become a trusted advisor, but, when you make that initial call, you are a vendor. You know what you can do for them, but they don't know. You are an interruption, possibly an annoyance. You have a big hurdle to get over right from the get-go. The only way to get over the hurdle is to immediately answer the prospect's internal question, "WIIFM?"

There is another sign that should go on your wall. This sign asks the question, "Why would anyone want to do business with me?" People will want to do business with you if, and only if, you can solve their problem. The pain they feel comes from a problem. You are the solution to the problem. If you can answer both of these questions, you will feel more confident when you make cold calls because you will know why you are the best person to help them. This gives you a psychological boost.

I admit, though, that even with this psychological boost and a great hook in your opener, cold calling is difficult. It is very difficult. Sure you know that you have to make x calls to get y appointments to make z sales. Sure you know that all those "no's" are just part of the numbers game. Sure you know that "no" is not a personal indictment of you. No matter what you know, however, cold calling is beastly hard. It's very easy to find excuses to not call.

Your excuses may be valid. It may be the day after Thanksgiving. Everyone may be at Grandma's eating leftover turkey and pumpkin pie. Call anyway. Your competitors probably won't call that day so you have a big advantage. Remember, 10% of the salespeople get 80% of the business. This could be your golden opportunity. Maybe the prospects won't be in the office. Maybe they won't talk to you if they are. Then again, maybe they will and you could open the door to a sale.

Getting the appointment is the hardest part of your job. You won't get the date unless the prospect has a reason to stop what he is doing to listen to you and agree to meet with you and it has to be a darn good reason since everyone already has more things to do than they could do if they lived to be 200. Unless the prospect judges that the possible benefits to be gained from listening to you might be greater than the value of the time he would be losing, you won't get an appointment. Your job in the cold call is to convince him that the benefit is so great he needs to talk to you. Almost nobody likes to make cold calls. Most people truly hate to make them, but, until you become Top Dog, The Expert, you are in survival mode and cold calling is necessary to survive long enough to succeed.

IF YOU SEND IT, WILL THEY READ IT?

The same strategy that you use in cold calls is the strategy that you would use for sales letters. Once again you have only a few seconds to grab the reader's attention. The survival rate of sales letters is approximately equal to the survival rate of cold calls. In both cases you have only seconds to create the desired, "Tell me more" response. To do that you have to immediately address the prospect's pain.

I usually read every letter I get because I coach people on how to make everything they do market them. I want to see how other people are marketing themselves. Even I have a limit, though. One day I opened my mail, read one-half of the first sentence and threw the letter into the wastebasket. The sentence began, "I pride myself on my...."

Who cares?! Nobody cares about you. They care about what you can do for them and you have to hook them with that information right away. People buy on emotion and later justify with logic so you have to reach out, emotionally grab them by the throat and give them a reason to listen to you. Later on they will want to know your credentials. That's when the logic part comes into play. The emotional response has to come first.

A common trouble spot for salespeople planning what they will say is recognizing the difference between benefits and features. Benefits are what your products and services do for your client. Features are how the products and services do it. Selling on features never works. Sell the benefits and let prospects justify their purchases with information about the features.

The purpose of a sales letter, as opposed to a direct mail letter, is to begin the prospect relationship, not to make an immediate sale. One successful tactic is to send a sales letter with an article from a magazine or newspaper that discusses a problem common to your target market. The letter should briefly introduce you, make reference to the problem discussed in the article and tell the prospect that you will call him the following week to set an appointment to show him how you have helped other people with the same problem. Make sure you do call the following week. Otherwise, your credibility with the prospect is zero.

If you call and don't get the appointment, continue to pursue the prospect with phone calls at regular intervals and with other letters or notes. The prospect relationship is the most overlooked part of selling. A "no" isn't a "no" forever. A "no" is a "no" for now. Even if it did turn out to be forever, a prospect can be an excellent referral source. I have been referred by prospects who never became clients.

WRITING THE SALES LETTER

Before you begin to write, write down the answers to these questions.

What are my prospects concerned about?
What do they desire?
What do they fear?
What needs can I fill?
How can I fill those needs?

Knowing the answers to these questions will help you plan the best way to approach your prospects.

Once you know what solution you will be offering, begin to formulate the solution in terms of benefits, not in terms of features. Features are characteristics of the products and/or services. For example, a telephone may be cordless. That is a feature. The benefit of a cordless phone is that the person using the phone will be able to move from the desk to the filing cabinet during the conversation rather than having to put the caller on hold while he searches for some information.

To see the distinction between benefits and features, take a sheet of paper and make two columns. In the left-hand column, list all the features of your service. In the right-hand column, opposite each feature, list the benefit the prospect will receive from that feature. The most important benefit on your list is the benefit that will appear in the first sentence of your letter. This is the sentence that has to reach out and grab the reader. Think of your opening sentence as a newspaper headline or the headline of an advertisement.

Questions are very effective opening sentences. "Are you worried about having sufficient funds for retirement?" "What would happen to your business if you died suddenly?" "Will you have enough money to send your children to college?" "Could you pay for long-term nursing care?" The longest running ad in our country had the headline, "Do you make these mistakes in English?" Your opening sentence is the headline of your sales letter.

Your opening sentence is the "hook" which grabs your reader and makes him want to read more. It has to immediately show him that you can satisfy a need that he has. "Immediately" is the operative word. You have no more than three seconds to grab the reader's attention. For example, if you are an insurance agent, an attention-grabbing headline would be, "One-third of homeowners will be sued at least once."

The only time you would not need a headline is when you have already had personal contact with the prospect. Then you would begin with a sentence that refers to that contact. "When we talked at the Rotary meeting last Thursday, you asked me to send you some information on annuities."

After the opening sentence your first paragraph should go on to develop the benefit. Remember, your reader is always asking WIIFM. Even with an opening that refers to a prior meeting, you still have to immediately go to the hook. Write three or four more sentences that describe the benefit to the reader. Use the most effective marketing word, "YOU."

Now, answer objections that the reader may have in his mind. To do this, take another sheet of paper and make two columns. In the left-hand column, list all the objections that a prospect might raise. In the right-hand column, write your answer to each objection. You want to raise and counter these objections in your letter.

For example, if you are selling a prepaid, one-year family portrait package, one objection might be, "It's too expensive." In your letter address this objection by stating, "These portrait sittings would cost 50% more if purchased separately."

Another objection might be, "If my children get sick or my husband is traveling a lot and we can't come for all of the sittings, I will have paid for something I didn't get." Address this objection in the letter by stating, "Any sittings not done during the calendar year will be scheduled at no additional charge the following year."

If you don't counter objections in the letter, they may be strong enough to keep you from getting an appointment with the prospect. The prospect is always looking for a reason to not do business with you, to not even meet with you.

The third part of planning your sales letter is to plan the conclusion. You should close with a call to action. The call to action tells the prospect what you want him to do after he reads your sales letter. Do you want him to call you? Do you want him to send for more information? Every sales letter should end with a call for action just as every direct mail letter does. Tell the reader specifically what you want him to do.

Exercise: Write your own sales letter.

First, write the opening sentence, the "hook."

Second, write the remainder of the first paragraph (three or four more sentences that develop the benefit you used as a hook in your opening sentence.)

Third, write two or three paragraphs that answer the main objections that you believe the reader might raise in his own mind.

Fourth, end with a short paragraph that calls the reader to take a specific action.

Fifth, add a P.S. to the end of your letter.

A P.S. that mentions a benefit the reader will receive when he acts will increase the likelihood of your getting a response to your letter.

Numbers one and five, the opening sentence and the P.S., are the parts of the letter that your prospect will read first. In fact, they may very well be the only parts that he reads. They have to be a strong answer to the question, "What's in it for me?" Everything you put in your letter has to sing your prospect's favorite song, WIIFM. Wiif-em with your words.

Once your letter is written and printed, go back and edit it. Look for awkward wording, unprofessional appearance, bad grammar, spelling errors. Check the length of the letter. It should be brief. Direct mail letters can, with the right market and the right product, be long and detailed. They are trying to sell on the spot. Sales letters should never be long. They are not trying to sell. They are merely trying to open the door for you to get to see the prospect.

After you have proofread the letter, have someone else proofread it. I am a careful proofreader, but I can't remember a time when, careful as I am, the other proofreader did not find at least one error.

After you and an independent reader proofread the letter and you make the necessary changes, proofread the letter again. Then, critique the letter as though you were your prospect. Ask yourself the following questions:

Is the letter professional?
Does the first sentence grab my attention?
Does it make me want to read more?
Does it offer me the solution to a problem that I know I have?
Does it tell me that I might have a problem that I didn't know I had?
Does it tell me how to take advantage of an opportunity?
Does it address objections I might have?
Does it ask me to do something?
Does it make me want to take some action other than
throwing it into the circular file?
Could the letter be improved?
How?
Does the letter have a P.S.?

Then, ask someone else to also critique the letter. He may not have depth knowledge of your business. That's fine. In fact, that is desirable. Your prospects don't.

Ask him what he would think if he got your letter in the mail. Would he respond? Why or why not? Of course, you will need to beg him to be brutally honest rather than kind. Better that he be brutally honest than that you send a bad sales letter. A bad letter "unmarkets" you. It can undo all the good you have done with your marketing efforts.

SALES LETTER FOLLOW-UP

A good sales letter may get you a response. Hopefully, it will get you lots of responses. In a perfect world the prospect would immediately respond to your call to action. He would call you to set an appointment or mail back the enclosed card for more information or fax the form to register for your seminar. That is in a perfect world.

In the real world the prospect has a million things all happening at once. He may throw your letter away unopened. He may put the letter aside. He may plan to call you or register for your seminar later, when he has more time. Your letter goes on the to-do pile or your number goes on the bottom of the call list. Maybe the prospect isn't even sure if he wants to respond so your offer goes into a file labeled

"Pending." Someday the file may be opened or it may just plain get lost under mountains of paperwork on the desk.

Because we live in the real world, not the perfect world, it is vital that you follow-up each letter that you send. Your follow-up has to be as effective as your letter. Otherwise you fall into the trap that is always waiting for us. You fall into the trap of "unmarketing" yourself.

To see how unmarketing works, think about the follow-up calls you have received. Of course, you can also think about the follow-up calls you didn't receive. Last year I responded to an offer for a free videotaping of my home for insurance purposes. The insurance agent spent an hour with me, did the taping and said she would be back to me in a week with a proposal for homeowners' insurance. She was confident she could beat the price of my current insurer. I didn't hear from her in a week. I didn't hear from her in a month. I didn't hear from her ever. I guess her company couldn't beat my current insurer's price. The correct thing to do would have been to call me, tell me that and offer to be of help to me in the future if I had any questions or became dissatisfied with the service I was receiving from my current insurer. By not responding she lost any potential business I might have sent her way, wasted an hour of her time and lost an opportunity to market herself. After all, someday she might end up working for another company that could beat the price of my current insurer. She "unmarketed" herself so, if that happens, she'll never know. She lost any chance of ever doing business with me and lost any referrals I might have given her. The cost of not making a phone call can be incredibly high.

If you are a good marketer and you do make a follow-up call, make your follow-up call effective. Haven't you received calls like this?

"Hi! This is Edwin Schroeder. I was just calling to see
if you got my letter and if you have any questions."

I don't know what you think when you get a call like this, but I say to myself,

"I think I saw it as I was throwing it into the recycle bin."

Of course I don't say that to Edwin. To Edwin I say,

"Yes, I got it. No, I don't have any questions."

Edwin usually then says,

"Oh. Well, if you do, feel free to call me."

I say,
"I sure will."
I mentally add, "the twelfth of Never."
What a waste of his time and mine!

Instead of asking me lamely if I had any questions, he should have referred back to the "hook" in his sales letter and used it to remind me that I have a pain he can fix. If he could have brought that pain to the front of my mind, he might still have been able to spark my interest. Every call needs to be a marketing call. Otherwise there is no point in making the call. What would you have thought of Edwin after you got his call? I thought he was inept, not very interested in getting my business and probably not capable of handling it if he did get it.

CHAPTER SIX

MAKING THE SALE

Once you have gotten this far, all of your marketing begins to pay off. Finally you are ready for Part Six of TDS, Making the Sale or, in Top Dog terms, *Becoming the Pick of the Litter*. Getting to the point of going on a sales call means your marketing has been successful. You have put a lot of time, money and expense into marketing yourself. You have probably done many or all of the following: written articles, given speeches, held seminars, networked, networked, networked, served on committees and boards, gotten interviewed, produced a newsletter, made innumerable cold calls and networked, networked, networked. Your fingers have frostbite. Your stomach literally cannot stomach another rubber chicken. You are bleary-eyed and exhausted.

The end is in sight, but you still have one more hurdle, the sales call. Making the sale is the only part of TDS that is selling. However, it is also marketing. The techniques you used in marketing yourself to get to the sales call are needed to successfully turn the appointment into a sale.

Just as in everything else you have done up until this point, you need a strategy. Every strategy is based on achieving specific objectives. Know your objectives for the sales call. Your initial appointment should have just two objectives, to establish rapport and to uncover a need you can satisfy in a way that you want to satisfy it.

The winning strategy for a sales call is based on asking a sequence of questions. This questioning sequence consists of a background question, a problem question, a consequence question and a solution question. This questioning sequence has two purposes. First, it uncovers the prospect's need. Second, it grows that need in the prospect's mind. It is the mental equivalent of a magnifying glass. When the problem is magnified, the price of the solution becomes minimized in the prospect's mind. When the problem is large enough and pressing enough, the prospect becomes more interested in how quickly you can solve it rather than in how much it will cost to solve.

The questions you ask provide the framework for the sales call. If you don't ask the right questions, you may as well not make the call. First, your questions should uncover basic information, the equivalent of the military's name, rank and serial number. Second, your questions should help you fish for problems that you can solve. What problems does the prospect recognize that he has? What problems can you see that the prospect may not see? Third, your questions should help you understand the scope of each problem. You want to discover what negative effect(s) the problem is having or could have on the person or the business. Fourth, your questions should show you and the prospect the cost of not solving the problem. What is the problem costing him now? If he doesn't solve it, how much more could it cost him? With enough questioning, the prospect will sell himself on the need for your services.

Ask:

What will happen if _____ isn't solved/fixed/changed?
What will happen if you don't have surgery on your rotator cuff?
What will happen if you don't make a will?
What will happen if you don't have the root canal done?
What will happen if you don't reduce employee theft?

Your goal is to probe for the pain and, then, help the prospect feel it. You follow the same strategy a doctor follows. You ask questions, make a diagnosis and, then, prescribe a treatment regimen. The one thing you don't do is talk. You listen.

Tip: Often salespeople talk 80% of the time and listen 20% of the time. It should be just the reverse. The more you talk, the less you sell. Molony's Law.

Your job in the initial sales call is to find the problem, analyze the problem and grow the problem in the prospect's mind until the cost of the problem is bigger than the cost of the solution. You may be able to do all of this in one sales call. If so, Hallelujah! It is more likely, though, that you will do your detective work in the first sales call and make the sale on the second or third or fourth call.

PREPARING FOR THE SALES CALL

Preparation is always the key to success. Set a goal. Know exactly the result you want to achieve during the call. Don't wing it. You are trying to be Top Dog, not Lame Duck.

This is the moment that you have been preparing for in all of your marketing to date. Preparation begins with researching the prospect. You already know the kinds of problems your clients have because you have thoroughly studied your target market. Now you need to study this individual prospect. Find out as much personal and/or business information about the prospect as you can. Does he have the same problems the rest of your target market has? Does he have any unique problems? Write out the questions you are going to ask to uncover these specific problems. Before you go on the sales call, review your research. You reviewed your research before you attended a networking event. It is even more important that you review your research now.

Exercise:

First, list the problems that your prospect probably has. You will know what they are because most of the people in your target market have the same problems.

Second, write down the questions that you will ask during the sales call to uncover each of the problems.

> TIP: Always be listening for a problem that you hadn't even considered. Being a good listener is simultaneously the most valuable and the most underutilized skill a person can have.

Most of your competitors will be preparing answers to the objections they expect to receive. By using a questioning strategy, you prevent the objections from arising in the first place. Use questions to uncover, understand and grow the pain and let the prospect sell himself on the solution.

Many salespeople rush in ready to sell a solution before the prospect feels the pain. When you approach a prospect, he is in the middle of doing something, maybe several things. His mind is probably not on the problem you want to solve for him. This means that you have to introduce the problem and grow it until he feels it.

Present the problem. Grow the problem. Help the prospect feel an urgency about solving the problem. Then, and only then, offer a solution. The more you make him feel it, the more he will want relief. Let the prospect sell himself.

Always sell to the pain. It is easier than selling to the pleasure. Let's use "customer satisfaction" as an example. Pleasure is increasing customer satisfaction. Pain is avoiding customer complaints and the loss of customers who choose to no longer do business with you. Pleasure is often intangible. Pain is measurable and very real.

Lost customers mean lost revenue, no referrals and bad word-of-mouth advertising which leads to more lost revenue. How much is your average customer worth a year? What is his lifetime value? What percentage of your business is business referred by current customers? What is the dollar value of that business a year? These questions can all be answered with numbers, cold, hard, concrete numbers.

A lost customer translates directly into x dollars of lost revenue. Pain is concrete so it is always easier to sell to the pain. The ad that opened with the question, "Do you make these mistakes in English?" played on the embarrassment the reader feels if he makes a grammatical error rather than talking about the better job he might get if he didn't make those errors. Pain is "now," in the present. Pleasure is often "then," in the future.

During a sales call the first thing you need to do is find out what the prospect's problems are. You can't be the solution if you don't know what the problem is. And you literally are the solution because you are not selling a product or service. You are not selling stocks, bonds or annuities. You are selling what those stocks, bonds and annuities can do for the client. You are selling a secure future.

As you use your questioning strategy, really listen. Listen. Listen. Listen. Then, listen some more. A good detective asks a question and, then, shuts his mouth and listens to the answer. We tend to talk ourselves out of sales. The heart of marketing is research and research is, in essence, nothing more than listening. No one ever listened himself out of a sale, but many people have talked themselves out of one. When we are talking, we aren't learning what the prospect wants and we are not allowing the prospect to sell himself.

Let the prospect talk. The 80/20 rule applies here, too. The prospect should be talking 80% of the time, minimum. You can't sell a solution if you don't know what the problem is. You can't find out what the problem is if you are talking. In addition, the more you talk, the greater the chance that you will talk yourself out of the sale. When you are talking, you are not building rapport. You are not building trust. You are not growing the problem in the prospect's mind.

I read a wonderful statement a while ago that sums this up beautifully. "He was finished half an hour ago. He just hasn't stopped talking yet." Another excellent quote is one that has been around for a long time. "Telling is not selling." We have two ears and one mouth for an excellent reason.

When you talk to someone, there are really two conversations going on at the same time. One conversation is the conversation between you and the prospect. The other conversation is the conversation the prospect is having with himself. If you are dominating the conversation with the prospect, he has even more time to devote to his internal conversation. Conversely, if he is talking to you, he can't be talking to himself.

During the sales call, help the prospect uncover his problem by using the questions you wrote down during your pre-appointment planning session. "Is your contact manager software difficult to use?" "Are you having problems saving money for your children's college education?" The beginning of a sales call is basically market research. What is the prospect's problem? How has he tried to solve the problem? How successful has he been?

After you uncover the problem, grow it in the prospect's mind to the point where the cost of the solving the problem is less than the cost of not solving the problem. As the list of new problems that could develop as a result of not fixing the current problem grows, the cost of fixing the problem appears to shrink.

The greater the number of consequences and the more strongly the prospect feels them, the less the cost of solving the problem is an issue. To uncover possible problems ask: "What is happening because of this problem? Is this problem creating other problems now? Could it create other problems in the future?"

Help the prospect feel the pain of not solving his problem. Help him want you. If your basement is flooding, you may not like the plumber's price, but you WANT his help. The pain of not solving the problem far outweighs the pain of paying the plumber's bill, especially at the time he is providing the service. One year we moved into a new home on September 3. Thanksgiving morning I walked into my kitchen to find water running down the wall, down the front of the microwave oven, across the counter, down the front of the lower cabinets and onto the floor.

The situation looked like this:

Situation: Water flowing into kitchen from second floor
Problem #1: Damage to cabinets
Problem #2: Damage to microwave oven, including possible destruction of microwave oven.
Problem #3: Damage to counters
Problem #4: Damage to floor
Problem #5: Damage to my serenity/composure/sanity,
i.e, barely-controlled hysteria
Problem #6: Inability to prepare and serve Thanksgiving
dinner for the extended family that was visiting

The pain of all of these problems outweighed the pain of paying double or triple time for a plumber on a holiday. The plumber didn't have to sell his services. My pain sold them. When you identify the problem and grow it until the prospect feels it, you won't have to sell him. He will sell himself.

You have to constantly be in intelligence-gathering mode. You should get all the information that you can get before you give any information. Be a detective. Ask questions. There is a proven correlation between the number of questions you ask and the number of sales you make. Ask as many open-ended questions as possible, questions like: "What process did you use in making that decision?" and "How do you select your trainers?" An open-ended question requires a complete answer. It cannot be answered with a simple, "Yes" or "No." The answers to open-ended questions allow you to probe for information. A question that can be answered "Yes" or "No" leads to a closed door. An open-ended question leads to an open door which leads to more open doors.

As well as uncovering his problems find out what the customer wants. Find out how he wants to buy. What problems did he encounter in the past when he tried to buy the services you offer? What criteria did he use in the past to select whatever it is you sell? Sell the way the prospect wants to buy rather than trying to make him buy the way you want to sell. This means concentrating on the prospect and on what he is saying, not on your canned sales pitch and on how you will counter objections. Sales scripts will always hurt you because the prospect doesn't know his part.

Instead find out how the prospect buys. Follow his buying strategy rather than trying to make him follow your selling strategy. Sell the way he wants to buy. Look at yourself through his eyes and see what you and your services look like to the prospect. There is an old saying that is as true today as it ever was.

> "To sell Jim Jones what Jim Jones buys,
> see Jim Jones through Jim Jones's eyes."

A word of warning: Even if it price is paramount to Jim Jones, do not sell on price. Never sell on price. You are not a vacuum cleaner. Top Dog doesn't sell on price. He sells on value. People pay for the best. Top Dog is the best.

There is a quiet assurance that the best salespeople radiate. They aren't worried about making the sale. They aren't trying to remember the magic closes they memorized or parroting a memorized script. Nothing approximates the sound of fingernails on a chalkboard as much as a canned script.

A successful salesperson follows the same procedure a doctor follows. A doctor is, first, a detective and, second, a healer. Your doctor doesn't sell. He advises. You advise. Your doctor asks you questions, diagnoses your problem and offers to help you, but he isn't trying to sell you. He is trying to heal you. A doctor asks, "What hurts? When? Where? How often? Has the problem gotten worse?" He tells the patient how to solve the problem and pictures the consequences of not solving the problem. In the same way you ask questions to diagnose the prospect's problem, grow it and help the prospect understand the consequences of not solving the problem.

In a perfect world every sales call would end with a sale. In the real world, it doesn't. Since making the sale is only one of four possible outcomes for a sales call, you have only a 25% chance that the appointment will end with a sale. The second possible outcome of your meeting is a definite, "No." The third possible outcome is an action step. An action step is a time-specific, people-specific step that the prospect agrees to take. An example of an action step is, "Let's meet again next Thursday at two." The fourth possible outcome is what I call "delusion." Delusion is believing the socially acceptable answers that the prospect gives to get you out the door without having to tell you he has no intention of buying. It is socially acceptable to say, "I'll think about it" or "I have to ask my accountant" or "I'll call you when things aren't so crazy around here." What he really means is "No," but he doesn't have the courage to say it.

Don't be deluded. Never leave a sales call harboring any illusions. If you receive a polite answer that is vague and sets no definite next step, assume it is a "no." In most cases it is. If you think of it as a "no," you will save yourself a lot of wasted effort and disappointment trying to sell someone who doesn't want to be sold. "No" is not the worst outcome of a sales call. Delusion is. In fact, "no" is good. It allows you to save your energy for prospects who will buy. Besides, a "no" isn't a "no" forever. A "no" is a "no" for now.

Whether you leave the appointment with a sale, a rejection or a mutually-agreed on action step, always send a handwritten note. To make sure you do it, have the envelope addressed and stamped. Then, write the note as soon as possible, perhaps even when you get in your car after the meeting. Definitely do it no later than the next day. The sooner you do it, the better the impression you make. Also, the sooner you do it, the more likely it is to get done. The longer you wait, the greater the chance that the note will enter "Gonna Land" and never get done. Gonna Land is the graveyard of good intentions.

Follow the note with a letter outlining the prospect's needs. Thank him for his time. This both brings closure to the sales call and reinforces what was said.

DEBRIEFING THE SALES CALL

The next step is a critically important step that most salespeople don't take. After the sales call is over, debrief it. List the things you learned about the prospect. What are his fears? desires? needs? Analyze the outcome of the call. If you got the sale, why? What tipped the scales in your favor? What behaviors do you want to repeat on your next sales call? If you don't know, ask. If you don't know why you got the sale, how are you going to do it again? You can't duplicate what you did if you aren't aware of what you did. Once you know why you got the sale and what actions you will repeat, ask yourself what other actions you could take that might make you even more successful.

If you didn't get the sale, why not? If you don't know, how can you prevent yourself from repeating the same behavior and losing other sales? What actions will you change for your next sales call? Success is created by adding one successful behavior on top of another successful behavior.

Debrief your questioning strategy. Count the number of questions you asked. Analyze the kinds of questions you asked. What percentage of the time did you talk? During the time you were talking, what percentage of the time were you asking questions? Did you make the connection for the prospect between the features of your service and the benefits to him? Did you say, "This is what feature xyz will do for you?" Did you identify the problem? Did you grow the problem? Did you develop the consequences (costs) of not fixing the problem? Did you find out how the prospect buys? Did you sell him that way?

Success breeds success. You will be successful if you repeat successful behaviors. You will be unsuccessful if you repeat unsuccessful behaviors. Debriefing allows you to identify the successful behaviors so that you can repeat them and the unsuccessful behaviors so that you can eliminate them.

CHAPTER SEVEN

MINING YOUR ASSETS

You are now ready for Part Seven, Mining Your Assets, aka *Collecting Bones*. Once the wedding is over it is time to build the marriage. Once the sale is completed, it is time to build the client relationship. It is also time to mine for assets and ask for referrals.

An often overlooked part of the process of building a 100% referral-based business is building prospect relationships. We hear about building customer relationships all the time. They are essential for our success, but prospect relationships can be valuable, too. Prospects will, hopefully, become clients. Even if they don't, prospects can become referral sources.

You begin creating a prospect relationship with your first phone call, your first introduction at a networking event, your first meeting. After the first meeting, the letter you send outlining the prospect's objectives helps build the relationship. So does your follow-up call to verify that you understood the prospects' objectives. Each contact is another link between you and the prospect. Every call. Every letter. Every handwritten note. Every article reprint you send. Every exposure helps guarantee that you will stay in the prospect's mind. It is a thread. The more threads you weave together, the stronger the rope. The more contacts you have, within reason, the stronger the relationship. You want enough contacts to stay in the prospect's mind, but not so many that he feels pressured.

These contacts are part of your over-all marketing strategy. Schedule phone and mail contacts on a regular basis, be it monthly, quarterly, semi-annually. The interval will vary with the individual prospect. Also, make occasional, unscheduled contacts. You may call just to say, "Hello." You may send personal notes, thank you notes, I-read-about-you notes, I-saw-your-name-in-the-paper notes, I-read-your-wonderful-article notes, I-enjoyed-your-speech notes. You may send congratulation cards, sympathy cards, birthday cards, anniversary cards, retirement cards, get well cards, happy new house cards. You may send clippings about the prospect, his spouse, his children, his grandchildren, his alma mater(s), his community service. With both prospects and clients you build relationships through regularly-scheduled contacts supplemented by unscheduled contacts as opportunities arise.

Every contact says, "Look at me." Every contact should be part of an ongoing campaign. Your scheduled contacts should be executed on schedule and recorded. Your unscheduled (spontaneous) contacts should also be recorded. What gets measured gets done. Recording your contacts is a way of measuring how well you are executing your contact strategy. If you don't have and faithfully use a contact strategy, when the prospect is ready to buy, one of your competitors will make the sale. If you don't maintain regular contact, when he is asked for a referral, a competitor will get the referral.

Of course, in order to have a contact strategy, you have to have a database. The prospect database is an abbreviated version of your client database. It has the same information except it will not have a purchase history. Prospects stay in the database until they become clients, die, move or tell you to stop contacting them. When they become clients, all of their information is transferred to the client database.

Since the prospect database is structurally the same as the client database, let's look at the client database. Your clients are your own personal gold mine, but, to work it, you need to know everything you can about them. The client database needs to contain the following information:

Demographic data:

Name
Address
Phone number(s)
Date of birth
Marital status

Education
Social security number, if necessary

Psychographic data:

Their interests
Their hobbies
Their travels
Their memberships
Their favorite charities
Their awards
Their likes
Their dislikes
Their goals
Their desires
Their fears
What they want
What they don't want

Relationship data:

Their relatives
Their friends
Their colleagues
Their neighbors
How/where/through whom you made the initial contact
What you discussed
Referrals you have received from them
Referrals you have given them

Transaction data:

Services you have provided
Services you are scheduled to provide
Possible future services that you have discussed with them

Your client database uses your prospect database as a foundation. You should start keeping both databases as soon as you have one prospect and one client. As your business grows it will become increasingly difficult to remember all the background information you gather on each person. Put it in the database. With a database you don't have to rely on your memory.

In addition to your databases you will need to maintain contact sheets. On the contact sheet you record when you contacted a prospect or client, how (by phone, fax, mail, e-mail, in person), what specifically was sent or discussed, what decisions were reached. We think we will remember all of this information, but it is humanly impossible once you have more than one or two prospects and one or two clients. Keep a record of all your contacts, including notes on meetings held, seminars attended, phone conversations and material mailed. The contact sheet should also include a history of referrals given and referrals received. These sheets go into a file with copies of all correspondence.

Building prospect and client databases is necessary. Following a schedule of regular contacts is necessary. Filling out contact sheets is necessary. However, all of these activities will get you nowhere if you don't do them consistently. You need to monitor your behavior so that you know if you indeed are having regular client and prospect contacts, keeping your databases current and keeping your contact sheets up-to-date.

To monitor my behavior I use an action chart. The action chart is a grid with a column for each of the activities I am supposed to be doing. I record the amount of time spent on each activity each day. At the end of the week I total the columns. It is a pain, but it tells me exactly how I am spending my time. I can't kid myself that I am marketing if my action sheet tells me I have spent a grand total of seventeen minutes on marketing for the week. I can't tell myself that I am writing an article for publication if I spent zero minutes working on it this week. I can't tell myself that I am prospecting if I made only three calls to prospects this week and sent out no sales letters. I can't tell myself I am nurturing client relationships if I called only one client this week just to say, "Hello" and sent no personal notes. The numbers in each column tell the truth. The tendency is to cut ourselves a little—or a lot—of slack. The numbers don't. They are what they are.

If I was scheduled to send handwritten notes to seven clients this week and I didn't, I am not following my client contact schedule. I can tell myself that I am building a database, but, if I did a seminar last week and have not added the prospects to my database, I am not building a database. If I have no entries in my contact sheets for yesterday and I was at work and contacted twelve prospects and two clients, then I am not maintaining my contact sheets. The numbers tell the truth. I either did or I didn't. I either am following my schedule of planned prospect and client contacts or I am not. If I'm not, I'm in Gonna Land. Top Dog wouldn't set a paw in Gonna Land because another name for Gonna Land is Loser Land. You either are or you aren't. Gonna doesn't count.

Regular contact is the lifeblood of a relationship, but contact alone isn't enough. Throughout the marriage you must court the client. You must nurture the relationship, constantly improving it.

Nurturing the relationship is critical to your success. Place your primary emphasis on nurturing your current clients rather than on finding new clients. Nurturing a relationship takes time, but economically it is the best thing to do.

You don't incur the marketing costs you would incur in wooing prospects. Your cost to nurture a relationship is a minor cost in your marketing budget. Nurture your current clients before you run off to find new ones. Would you walk away from a gold mine that was producing gold to go look for one somewhere else that might? Why would you go to the additional expense and effort? When you have a gold mine, get more gold from it.

How do you nurture your relationships? You have to court your clients. Always try to please them. Be grateful for a client's business and respectful of him. This seems too obvious to need stating, but, sadly, it isn't. Have you ever been taken for granted as a customer? Have you ever been treated rudely? Have you ever had a salesperson make you feel dumb? My husband and I became former customers of a luggage store after the owner tried to make us feel dumb. She didn't succeed. She simply made us angry.

My husband told the owner of the store the story of how our luggage had been damaged. She laughingly asked, "And what did you do? Nothing, right?" The owner laughed her way out of a sale of four suitcases. We went directly across the street to her competitor. I was delighted to take my business elsewhere. It would have been so easy for her to be courteous to us. The basic rule of good business is to listen to your customers and respect them. You don't have to agree with them. All you have to do is treat them the way you would like to be treated. It is mind-boggling the number of businesses that don't understand this most basic tenet of human interaction.

Losing a customer through poor service or rudeness isn't just foolish. It is business suicide. Your greatest profit comes from repeat business. With repeat business you have no marketing costs. With repeat business you have a greatly reduced expenditure of time. Building long-term relationships is the best marketing you can do. Often too much time and money is spent getting the customer and not enough time and money is spent keeping the customer. That is the classic marketing error.

"A rose is a rose is a rose," but, "a customer is not a customer is not a customer." It costs you five times more to get a customer than it does to keep a customer. A new customer each year for five years will not spend the same amount as a current customer during the same five-year period. In addition, on top of the future revenue you lose when you lose a customer, there is all the revenue you will never get from people who decide not to do business with you after they hear your dissatisfied customer's story.

Keeping customers is more important than ever. The sales game has changed. Instead of the old transaction-oriented selling with the emphasis on a string of single transactions with a long list of customers, selling has now become relationship-oriented selling where the emphasis is on a series of transactions with a single customer. The focus is on the customer's lifetime value, on lowering the cost of acquiring customers, on increasing the revenue from each sale. The most expensive way to generate a sale is to acquire a new customer. It is far more profitable to get a current customer to buy more, to buy more often and to convince his friends to buy from you.

Too often, however, we are so busy chasing future customers, that we aren't nurturing our current customers. What happens? Of the customers we lose, 66% stop doing business with us because they are dissatisfied with our service. We will always lose clients. They die. They become incapacitated. They move away. Their friends or their children or their children's spouses become dentists or doctors or lawyers or attorneys or decorators or accountants. We will always lose some. But, 66% of the customers we lose we don't have to lose.

AT &T conducted a two-year study of the reasons customers stopped doing business with a company. These were the results:

1% die
3% relocate
10% have other associations
19% prefer another vendor
24% have had a bad experience
42% just felt "no one cares"

The customers who left because they had a bad experience and the customers who left because they felt unappreciated totaled 66% of those customers who were lost. They didn't have to be lost. Another 19% might have been kept or won back if the company found out what the other vendor was doing better.

How do your clients feel about you? Even when prospects become clients, you need to continue doing market research. Are they delighted with your service? Dissatisfied? Do you know? Your competitors, if they're doing market research, are asking these same questions. Your clients are certainly always asking themselves whether or not they are pleased with your services. You need to put an intelligence-gathering system in place that will allow you to know the answers to these questions. If you know how your clients feel, you can hold onto the majority of them, thereby saving the time and effort and money you would need to put into chasing new clients to replace them.

Make gathering customer intelligence a priority. Constantly ask your clients, as Ed Koch asked the voters when he was mayor of New York City, "How am I doing?" Beg them to complain. If your clients know that complaining will help you, they will be able to get over the "nice person" hurdle and give you the negative feedback you need. Customer intelligence is more important than competitor intelligence. What your competitor is doing is important. What your clients think of what you are doing is far more important.

You can gather customer intelligence by asking questions like:

> What am I doing that you like?
> What am I doing that you don't like?
> What do you wish I did in a different way?
> What do you wish I didn't do?
> What am I not doing that you wish I did?

Make a list of how you think your clients would answer and, then, ask your clients. Compare the answers you thought you would get with the answers you did get. You may be very surprised.

Find out what is wrong and fix it. Bad word-of-mouth will destroy you. Most customers don't complain. They walk and, then, they talk. It is far better if they talk to you so they won't walk. You can't fix a problem if you don't know it exists. Finding a problem and fixing it is very good for your relationship with the client. The most loyal customer is one who had a problem that was fixed to his satisfaction. Interestingly, a customer with a problem made right is even more loyal than a customer who never had a problem.

You will always lose clients. Most of the clients you lose, though, you don't have to lose and don't want to lose. Always losing and looking is costly and time-consuming. To save time and money continue marketing to current clients. Marketing to current clients is part of the marriage. Marketing should have a dual focus, internal and external. Too often, however, we focus almost exclusively on marketing to our prospects instead of marketing as much or more to our clients. Marketing should never stop, just like the courtship should never stop. When you start taking your clients for granted, they can easily be wooed into the waiting arms of your competitors.

Constantly nurturing the relationships you have built ensures that you will keep most of your clients. Maintaining regular contact and providing excellent service are two ways that you tell clients that you appreciate them and their business. There is also a third way that is equally important. To keep clients you have to not only create value for them, but you have to also show them the value you are giving them. Do your clients know the full value they are deriving from their relationship with you? Being valuable isn't enough if the client doesn't realize how valuable you are. Document what you have done for them and give them written progress reports that show how they have benefited from their relationship with you. Then, talk to them about those benefits. If they don't see the number of benefits that you see, they can't appreciate the value of your service.

Creating and proving value is at the heart of the client relationship. You are continuing to market yourself to your clients when you show them the value you bring to the relationship.

Always look for ways you can make your services even more valuable. What else can you do for them? If your customer intelligence-gathering revealed needs that you are not filling, if possible begin to fill the needs. If the answers to your questions revealed any areas of dissatisfaction, remedy them, if you can.

One of the best ways to increase your value to your clients is to be their information resource. You used education as a marketing tool to get them. Now use it as a tool to keep them. Education sources are always considered valuable.

After you have established, nurtured and built value in the client relationship, you can begin to mine it. This is the last step in TDS, *Mining Your Assets*. First, build the relationship. Second, nurture the relationship. Third, show value in the relationship. Fourth, mine the relationship.

There are two different ways to mine a relationship. You can increase the revenue that you are getting from the client and you can bring in new revenue through referrals to the client's friends, family, colleagues and influencers.

To do this you need a systematic method to increase revenue from your existing client base. Look for other services you can offer your clients. Cross-sell to your clients, particularly your affluent clients. For example, a financial advisor may have only 20% of an affluent client's assets. The other 80% are assets he doesn't have. This shows the importance of cross-selling and upselling clients. A simple example of cross-selling is the clothing salesperson who sells the customer a tie to go with his new suit. At the same time he sells him a more expensive suit than he planned on buying. That's upselling. What other services can you offer?

The second way to mine your clients is to build relationships with their families, friends, colleagues and influencers. You want to serve your client's needs. You also want to serve the people they know. In addition to building relationships with the families and friends and colleagues of your prospects and clients, build relationships with their influencers. Sometimes influencers are not obvious. When we think of influencers, we tend to think of attorneys, accountants and doctors, but there are many less obvious influencers in many markets. Some examples would be the ombudsman in a retirement community, the head of a trade association and the director of an athletic club.

The last step in building a 100% referral-based business is to ask for referrals to your clients' networks. This is obvious and, yet, surprisingly it often is not done. We hope for referrals. We pray for referrals. We are grateful for referrals. But often we do not ask for them. This goes back to our reluctance to market ourselves, our reluctance to say, "Look at me!" It definitely is an example of our fear of rejection. But, as the old saying goes, "If you don't ask, you don't get." We have all been hounded for names by pushy marketers. But, remember, you are not a pushy marketer. You are a professional providing a valuable service.

To prepare yourself to ask, do the following exercise:

If you have done a superior job for a client, talk about the work you did for him and the benefits he received. Tell him that you are available to consult with his friends if they have any concerns and would like a sounding board. The best time to broach the subject is when he is telling you how pleased he is with the work you have done.

You don't want to appear hungry. Top Dog never does. On the other hand, you don't want to appear so full that your clients think you don't want referrals. Right from the beginning, let them know that yours is a referral-based business. Set the expectation in their minds that they will give you referrals.

You get what you give. One of the best ways to get referrals is to give them. Give referrals to your clients who own their own businesses. If you are a referral source for them, they will often reciprocate and become a referral source for you. It adds to the value of their relationship with you and strengthens the bonds that tie you together, making it more difficult to break those bonds and take their business elsewhere because you are helping them in more than one way.

Cultivate referrals from centers of influence. If you don't have clients that can use their services, but you would like them to refer their clients to you, find out what else they need. You may not have referrals for them, but you may be able to offer them something else of value. Perhaps you can get them PR in the publications that their target markets read. You could write an article about them or hire someone else to write it. The goal is to help them market themselves. You then become a valuable part of their marketing strategy.

You can help influencers grow their businesses by becoming an implicit referral source for them. Organize a seminar and ask one of your influencers to be the presenter. This gives him a chance to present at no charge and to gain new clients. It also helps to bind him to you and to encourage referrals. Other people may be able to provide the services you provide. However, they may not give him the help marketing himself that he gets from you.

Remember, everyone is your marketing department. Make sure they understand your customer profile and how your clients benefit from working with you. Also, make sure that they know you are seeking referrals. Your clients know you are successful and busy. You have worked hard to create the perception of yourself as The Expert. Make sure that they also know that most of your business comes through referrals.

As with every other part of your marketing strategy, set goals for your process of asking for referrals. Your goals should be based on the actions you take, not on the results you get. Therefore, don't set a goal of getting ten more referrals this quarter. Instead, figure out how many requests you need to make to get ten referrals. Then, make asking that number of times your goal. If you need to make forty requests to get ten referrals, making forty requests should be your goal. You can't control how many times you will be given referrals. You can control how many times you ask for referrals.

When you discuss referrals, the work you have done to establish yourself as the expert will pay off. If you have established yourself as the expert, your referral sources will feel more confident about referring you.

As soon as you are given a referral immediately thank the referral source. Then, do some prospect research. Ask questions to find out as much as you can about the person being referred. Ask the referral source how long he has known the person and how well he knows him. Ask how he thinks you could help the person being referred.

Finally, ask your client to help you connect with the person being referred. If your client, Jeanette, tells you that you should call Denny, ask if she would be willing to contact Denny first and let him know that she has suggested you call him. Her call will ensure that your call is a warm call, not a cold call.

After you have contacted Denny, call Jeanette and thank her for her referral. After you actually meet with Denny, send Jeanette a handwritten note and, possibly, a small gift. It is important that the gift be small because many companies have strict rules about the cost of gifts their employees can accept. Gifts that are normally acceptable are books, candy, flowers and movie passes.

You are ALWAYS marketing yourself. Your clients don't know the value you are providing if you don't tell them. Providing value and having clients recognize your value are two different things. Therefore, you have to constantly increase your visibility, build your credibility and create your desirability with your clients just as you did when your clients were prospects. Your process of ongoing exposures shouldn't end when a prospect becomes a client any more than courtship should end after the wedding. You build your relationship on the value you provide.

Conclusion

TDS, the Top Dog System, is, at heart, simply a four-step process:

Target
Research
Approach
Follow-up

In a nutshell, do the right things and do things right.

Systems that are hard-to-understand don't work because people can't use them. Systems that are hard-to-follow don't work because people won't use them. This system is easy-to-understand and easy-to-use. All you need is desire and determination and drive.

You might want to go to Los Angeles. That's desire. You might plan on going to Los Angeles, no matter what. That's determination. Without the drive, however, you will literally sit in your driveway spinning your wheels while your competitors speed past you.

To reach your goal, you have to drive yourself to Los Angeles. TDS is a step-by-step process to get you there. It tells you how to work the car, where to drive it, when to drive it, where to stop and what to do when you get there. In the end, though, you have to drive.

Many salespeople have desire. They want to be #1, Top Dog. They have determination. They're gonna do it and gonna and gonna and gonna. The problem is that they never get off their "gonna" and drive themselves.

Do you want to be Top Dog? Sure. If you didn't, you wouldn't be reading this book.

Do you believe in your most secret heart of hearts that you can be Top Dog?

Here is where many salespeople sabotage themselves. Deep down, where no one else can see, they don't believe they can be Numero Uno, #1, Top Dog.

If I had to sum up in just one sentence my philosophy of why life turns out as it does, it would be:

> What you believe you are is what you are.

If you don't believe, right down to the molecules in your toes, that you can be something, you will never be it. You will sabotage yourself. You will blame the markets, the economy, your clients, your prospects, your boss, your co-workers, your spouse, your children, your lack of education, your.... etc., etc., etc., ad nauseum.

There will always be a plausible, tell-the-world reason. There will also always be the real, bottom-of-your-gut reason. And that reason is—always—that you didn't believe you could do it.

With TDS you can do it. Like Top Dog, you have learned the secret to success. There is no secret. Success comes from believing in yourself, having a process that works and working the process. TDS works. Follow it and your clients will follow you right to the ringing cash register.

No one else can do what you can do. No one. Work the system and your success will prove it.

978-0-595-43693-4
0-595-43693-5

www.ingramcontent.com/pod-product-compliance
Lightning Source LLC
Chambersburg PA
CBHW021543200526
45163CB00015B/863